About the Author

Dr. CHUANG-YE HONG is a renowned physician-scientist, medical educator and hospital administrator of international caliber. He holds a medical degree in Taiwan and a PhD from the University of London in the UK. His research on human sperm motility and Chinese herbal drugs were leading in the world. An Ig-Nobel Prize from USA was awarded to him for his interesting work on Coke and sperm. In addition to a distinguished career in academic medicine, he had business experience as CEO of a biotechnology company in China. He travelled extensively and wrote tirelessly. He is currently a Chair Professor at Taipei Medical University and consultant physician at Wan-Fang Hospital in Taiwan.

Encounters

with

Medicine

and

Sperm

A Taiwanese doctor,

an interesting and exciting life

no matter where he was

Chuang-Ye Hong

Matador
9 Priory Business Park,
Wistow Road, Kibworth Beauchamp,
Leicestershire. LE8 0RX
Tel: (+44) 116 279 2299
Fax: (+44) 116 279 2277
Email: books@troubador.co.uk
Web: www.troubador.co.uk/matador

ISBN 978 1784623 012 paperback
ISBN 978 1784623 449 hardback

British Library Cataloguing in Publication Data.
A catalogue record for this book is available from the British Library.

Typeset in 11pt Aldine401 BT Roman by Troubador Publishing Ltd, Leicester, UK

Matador is an imprint of Troubador Publishing Ltd

Dedicated to Fumi

Contents

Preface

Caesar proudly declared: 'I came, I saw, I conquered.' Not being a warrior, I uttered: 'I came, I saw, I heard.' In this book, I have recorded what I saw and heard during the past 65 years, for 40 of which I practised medicine.

Commitment to medicine was a tradition in my family and I experienced various encounters during different stages of my professional life – some exciting and some disappointing. No matter where these events happened – in Taiwan, China, England or America – they taught me lessons that some others might be interested to share.

While my medical career was guided by a determination to be a good physician and teacher, my encounter with human sperm motility was serendipitous: full of fun but totally unexpected. It was a highlight of my pioneering research, which I believed should be an endeavor driven by curiosity.

The publicity surrounding my Ig Nobel Prize in 2008 was half amusing and half satirical. Like many other encounters in my life, I had no other choice than to accept and enjoy it.

I extended the span of this book to include my ancestors' settlement in a small village on the southeast coast of China eight hundred years ago, about the time St. Bartholomew's Hospital, where I studied, was first built, and Cambridge University – from which my daughter graduated – had just been founded.

History is a record of human encounters. I wrote this book with the sense and sensibility of history. It is unlikely that I could leave a legend that lasted for millennia like Caesar, but I present here to current and future international readers the true story of a Taiwanese medical doctor of this century.

Acknowledgements

I owe thanks to my wife, Fumi for her great support in my writing of this book and in our lives together for nearly four decades.

Dr. Tien-Chun Chang, professor of medicine at National Taiwan University Medical College, and my brother-in-law, was the first to read this book. His daughter, Dr. Lin-Chau Chang, a meticulous pharmaceutical scientist, read the manuscript carefully and corrected many errors in my first draft.

Chang-Shi Lin, who immigrated to Japan with a Japanese name, Hyashi Shose, is my friend since childhood. He pushed me very hard to write this book. His critique was always sharp and to the point.

I express my sincere thanks to many with whom I had encounters. Their roles in enriching the contents of this book can be read in various chapters. In addition, I would like to mention two special couples.

My parents-in-law, Chang-Chi Wang and Shui-Yun Chang Wang, educated their daughter to be a dutiful wife and a caring mother. Fu-Chin Hung and Yueh-Kuei Lin Hung, parents of my son-in-law, were always graceful and generous. Without their assistance to my family, I could not have managed my demanding jobs smoothly and find spare time for writing.

This book could not successfully have been published without Sam Jordison, who not only gave me valuable advice during his assessment of the manuscript but also polished my prose style and standardized my sentences. Nikki Holt guided me through the labyrinth of the publishing industry. Jennifer Liptrot was the production manager of this book. She designed the cover with her artistic instinct. I would also like to thank Joe Shih who drew the maps and Lawrence Weiju Lin for his assistance in preparing the illustrations.

PART ONE

The Formative Years for Fathers and Sons

CHAPTER 1

An Early History of Taiwan.
My Ancestors Cross the Strait.

Taiwan is an island lying off the southeast coast of China. The ancestors of most Taiwanese people, including my own ancestors, moved to Taiwan from Fukien. Fukien is a province of mainland China which is separated from Taiwan by the 150-kilometers-wide Taiwan Strait.

Until the 17th century, Taiwan had been considered by the Chinese as a wild, disease-ridden island, unsuitable for habitation. The aborigines who lived there had genetic traits close to indigenous southern Pacific islanders. They were divided into several tribes; some lived in flat lands and some in high mountains. The modern history of Taiwan only started when the Dutch East India Company built a fortress in 1624 and began to trade with the aborigines on the south of the island.

The first wave of organized Chinese immigration to Taiwan started after the Ming dynasty fell. In 1644, a group of rebels attacked Beijing, the capital of the Ming Empire. Prior to this disaster, many starving peasants had joined the revolt, demonstrating their resentment of the government. The last Ming emperor hanged himself at Coal Hill, a small park at the back of the royal palace. Before taking his own life, he forced his queen to commit suicide and he killed his daughters with his sword.

At the same time, there was a strong army of Manchurians waiting outside the Shanhaiguan, or Mountain and Sea Pass, at the eastern end of the Great Wall. For more than 2,000 years, that 6,000-kilometers-long fortification had been an invincible defense used by the Chinese to prevent attacks from barbarians of the north. The Manchurians, living in northeast China outside the Great Wall, were thought to be such barbarians. Skilful in hunting and horse riding, they were fierce fighters in battlefields. And this was their long-awaited moment for a full-scale invasion of China.

A Ming general whose duty was supposed to have been to fight against the Manchurians opened the gate and let his former enemy pass through. He had helped them because he needed their help to save his concubine trapped in Beijing. The Manchurians soon smashed the rebellious peasants, but they did not go back to their homes outside the Great Wall. They wanted to stay inside and become rulers forever. And so, the Qing dynasty was established. It lasted for 287 years, until it was replaced by a republic in 1911.

Many remnants of the old Ming regime refused to bow to the new Qing emperor. Several armies were raised to fight against the Manchurians; one solider among them was Cheng-Gong Zen, a native of Fukien. His mother was Japanese, while his father, a merchant and pirate, dominated trading in the southeast coast of China. His father surrendered to the Qing dynasty, but he did not. He was furious that his mother had committed suicide after refusing to submit to the Qing soldiers. He decided to take Taiwan, making it a stronghold to retaliate against the Manchurians. In 1661, 25,000 men followed him. In a fleet of 200 ships, they sailed for Taiwan. His army laid siege to the Dutch fortress for nine months before the Dutch governor surrendered.

Cheng-Gong Zen and his son then ruled Taiwan for 22 years. His continuous resistance against the Qing regime resulted in the execution of his father in Beijing. In 1683, the Qing emperor sent an army to cross the Taiwan Strait and conquer Taiwan.

Worried that this island might someday become rebellious again, the Qing government imposed strict regulations on the immigration of Chinese to Taiwan. For some time, only men were allowed to go. This policy resulted in a large number of children being born to Chinese fathers and aboriginal mothers.

In the 19th century, millions in southern China died during the Taipin uprising, which was an attempt to overthrow the imperial court of Qing. Corruption was commonplace among Qing officers. The government paid a huge compensation to Western superpowers each time the Chinese army lost a war. Many poverty-stricken Chinese left their country to seek a better life abroad. A great number of them, particularly those from southern Fukien, migrated to southeast Asian nations such as Malaysia, Thailand, Vietnam and the Philippines. Taiwan was also a favorite and convenient destination for them.

Early Chinese immigrants preferred to settle down in the fertile and flat land of southern Taiwan. Rice, sugar cane and pineapple were major agricultural products. In the 19th century, tea leaves grown in the northern hills also became famous exports. Political and business centres moved north to Taipei. Many foreign businessmen opened offices in Taipei.

My great grandparents immigrated from a small village in Quanzhou, Fukien to Taiwan in the 1880s. My great grandfather, Bao-Xu Hong, ran a business selling rice in the old town of Taipei. Many residents and shop owners there were immigrants from Quanzhou. He chatted with his friends in the courtyard of the Longshan Temple.

Longshan meant 'Dragon Mountain' in Chinese. This Buddhist temple, built in 1738, was a place of worship as well as a gathering centre for the locals, who spoke in the dialect of Southern Fukien. The life style here was very similar to that in Quanzhou.

My great-grandfather passed away aged 54 in 1894.

Quanzhou means 'spring state' in Chinese. Around 1,000 years ago it was one of the most important ports in the world; it was the starting point of the sea leg of the Silk Road. Ships sailed from here to destinations as far as Arabia and India. Marco Polo embarked from here on his return journey to Venice in 1292, for instance. But its function as a centre for international trading faded gradually, because China became less interested in seeking power on the sea in the following centuries. In the 19th century, nearby city Xiamen flourished as the most important seaport in Fukien. The British asked the Chinese to open Xiamen as a treaty port and built a settlement there. Xiamen was better known as Amoy to many Europeans. Its neighboring villages of Zhangzhou, like those in Quanzhou, housed many Chinese immigrants in Taiwan and southeast Asian countries.

In 1894, the Japanese defeated the Chinese navy and the army of the Qing dynasty. The following year, the Chinese emperor sent the most trusted minister of his court to Japan to negotiate a peace treaty. Japan requested that China ceded Taiwan. China complied, considering this isolated island of little importance to its empire.

When the news spread to Taiwan, a number of notable and wealthy citizens began to worry about their uncertain future. Without getting consent from the emperor, they declared the foundation of a democratic Taiwanese Republic. Ching-Sung Tang, the Qing governor in Taiwan, acted as the president of the new republic and 20,000 soldiers of the Qing garrison in Taiwan were hired. It was the first republic in Asia that decided to resist Japanese occupation with its own forces.

The Japanese army landed in the northeast coast of Taiwan. They crushed all resistance on their 50-kilometer march to the capital city, Taipei. The retreating Chinese soldiers fled inside the city walls and started to loot and run riot in the streets. Citizens looking for a restoration of order sent volunteers to help the Japanese. They opened the city gate and let the Japanese smoothly enter the city in June 1895.

Knowing that the Japanese were approaching, President Tang and his close aids boarded a European merchant ship in Tamsui, a seaport west of Taipei. Abandoned soldiers fired from the shore, trying to block the ship's departure and asking for the salaries owed to them. The Englishmen mediated in this dispute before the steamer was allowed to sail for mainland China. The soldiers in Taipei put down their arms and returned to China with the agreement of the Japanese.

The resistance was much stronger when the Japanese moved southward. It was only after sending for reinforcements that they were able to control the whole island. It was seven months after their first landing. From the two million inhabitants of Taiwan, 20,000 had died in heroic fighting.

At this time of restlessness, some Taiwanese wondered whether they should go back to their hometowns in mainland China. Among them was the 28-year-old elder brother of my grandfather Ran Hong, who was only eight. Between these two there was another brother aged 14. My grandfather was born in Taipei, but his parents and two brothers were all born in Quanzhou. My grandfather was the first member of this family born in Taiwan.

My grandfather and his eldest brother boarded a small ship bound for Quanzhou. Another brother stayed in Taipei to take care of their mother. They wanted to know if the whole family should move back to mainland China. Conditions in their hometown were worse than they had expected. Life was hard and people poor. The news from Taipei, on the other hand, was encouraging. Taipei was peaceful. The Japanese worked hard to develop Taiwan into a model colony. The brothers realized that if they did not return to Taiwan in time, they would soon be denied residential rights there. They boarded a ship again. This time, they were on a journey of no return. A century later, would an offspring of theirs be able to visit their hometown in Quanzhou?

CHAPTER 2

The Japanese Improve Hygiene.
My Grandfather Studies Bacteria.

Infectious diseases caused by bacteria and parasites were leading causes of death before drugs to treat them were developed in the 20th century. The Japanese lost 160 soldiers in military action during the seven months they spent clearing the island-wide resistance of Taiwanese, but in the same time they lost 4,600 people to various diseases – mostly infectious ones. Partly for their own sake, the Japanese made improvements in hygiene and health a top priority.

Many episodes of dreadful infections swept Taiwan, in spite of the actions taken to improve health, including malaria, cholera, smallpox, typhoid, tuberculosis, syphilis, dysentery and plague. At the end of the 19th century, a severe plague started in southern China and spread to Taiwan. In the following years, 30,000 Taiwanese were infected; 24,000 of those died. The death rate was 80%.

The Japanese colonial government opened modern hospitals and trained the Taiwanese to become doctors. A medical school was founded by the Office of the Governor-General in 1899, four years after the Japanese took over Taiwan. At first, Taiwanese parents hesitated to send their children to the school. Only one student got his diploma when it had its first graduation. But very soon, it became the first choice when young Taiwanese were considering their career options. The Japanese encouraged the Taiwanese to learn practical subjects such as medicine, teaching and agriculture. Medical doctor and teacher were the two most respected professions in Taiwan. They were helpful to the colonial government in promoting islanders' health and Japanese culture. On the other hand, it was difficult for the Taiwanese to study law, politics or social sciences. If they planned to do so, they had to travel to Japan. The Japanese were suspicious of those who might lead their fellow Taiwanese to challenge Japanese administrative authority.

At first, boys completing primary school were allowed into the medical schools. Then they were required to have a diploma from a secondary school. This was after the name of the medical school was changed to Taipei Medical Professional School. When Taipei Imperial University was founded and the medical school was incorporated into the university, only those who completed a university preparatory school were accepted.

Before the Japanese came to Taiwan, most Taiwanese sought out Chinese herbal doctors when they had ailments. A few missionary doctors provided Western-style treatment, but only a limited number of patients had access to such a service.

In Japan, the practice of traditional Chinese medicine was abolished following the full-scale Westernization of the Meiji restoration in 1868. Many Japanese medical doctors went to Europe, Germany in particular, for advanced training. Likewise in Taiwan, the Japanese suppressed traditional Chinese medicine and taught Western medicine. Public hospitals provided only Western medicine.

Bacteriology was the medical discipline that progressed best at the turn of the 20th century. Louis Pasteur in Paris and Robert Koch in Berlin founded the theory for the pathogenesis of bacteria, and discovered causative agents for lethal diseases such as tuberculosis and cholera. They were worshiped as new saviors of mankind. Bacteriology research flourished worldwide. A key function of the Research Institute for the Office of Governor-General in Taiwan was the study of bacteriology and public health. This institute was built next to the medical school; most of its senior staff was made up from Japanese professors in the medical school.

My grandfather lost his beloved brothers a few years after he returned from Quanzhou. Both brothers died young and left no children – they all succumbed to epidemic infections. He decided to study bacteriology and joined the Research Institute after completing his studies of veterinary medicine in the agricultural school.

In 1911, a short but energetic Tsong-Ming Tu stepped into the bacteriology laboratory at the Research Institute for the Office of Governor-

The Japanese Improve Hygiene. My Grandfather Studies Bacteria.

9

General in Taiwan. He was a 19-year-old second-year medical student. He wanted to spend his summer vacation there learning how to cultivate bacteria for research. Tu met the Japanese chief of the laboratory, and the latter introduced Tu to a young Taiwanese man only a few years older than Tu. This young man, my grandfather, was an assistant in the laboratory. The chief advised Tu to learn experimental technologies from my grandfather. From then on, these two Taiwanese developed a lifelong friendship.

My great grandparents had arranged a marriage for my grandfather when he was still a boy. It was not an uncommon practice for two families to bolster their friendship by arranging their children to marry each other; this was of course without the consent of their children. Pointing to the pregnant woman's belly and thus booking a future son-in-law or daughter-in-law was an extreme example of such a custom.

My grandmother, Chen-Gu Hong, came from a wealthy family. One of her brothers was the most distinguished lawyer in Taipei. She was four years younger than my grandfather. Uniquely among girls of her age, she could read and write, and had trained as a midwife. She had refused to have her feet bound, and her open-minded father had agreed with her. Foot-binding was an old custom in China. Girls born to well-to-do families were forced to have their feet bound with long clothing so their walking with small but deformed feet could be more attractive to men. This cruel torture to women was abolished after the fall of the Qing dynasty.

My grandfather in his early adulthood had neither a father nor a brother; he lived with a widowed mother. Life with him had the potential to be tough, but the parents of my grandmother kept their promise to their old friend and let my grandfather marry their daughter.

The first child of my grandparents was a girl. They named her Zhao-Di, or bring in a brother. The second was again a girl, this time called Yue-Di, or happy to have a brother. This showed how eager they were to have a son.

Their wish came true. The third one was a boy. A new child then came every third year. They had a total of five sons. My father, Li-Chau Hong was their fourth son.

In order to help meet the medical needs of the islanders, the Japanese health authority issued a special medical license to those who did not attend medical school, but had certain experience in medically related fields and passed an examination. The number of annual graduates from the medical school was too small to meet the huge demand. My grandfather was given such a license. Medicine was much better paid than laboratory work. He was not moved. He loved medical research and stuck with it.

In 1915, the Taiwanese Medical Association was founded. It was the first professional medical organization in Taiwan. Its official journal was edited by Japanese professors at the medical school. My grandfather was listed as the author of 10 papers for this journal during its first 10 years. Few Taiwanese names appeared in this journal at that time. A first-generation medical scientist in Taiwan, he was later granted a doctoral degree from the University of Kyoto in Japan.

After completing medical school, Tu did not go into medical practice to enjoy a lucrative income. He went to Kyoto, where he studied pharmacology and became the first Taiwanese who ever received a doctoral degree. Returning to Taipei, he immediately met my grandfather. Together, they studied the toxicity of yam in animals and co-authored a paper. This was not only the first paper from Tu in Taiwan, but also the start of his research on Chinese herbal drugs. Tu chose opium addiction, snake venom and Chinese herbal drugs as his major research topics.

Opium-smoking was common and legal among Chinese people in the late Qing dynasty. Many of them fell into poverty because they spent their fortune buying this poison. Opium damaged their health – they became physically and mentally weak. The colonial government banned it in Taiwan, but issued a special permission allowing those Taiwanese who had been addicted before the announcement to continue smoking. Tu and his students engaged in laboratory and clinical studies of opium, including how to help the addicted to refrain from it.

Snakes were once easy to find and catch in the bushes and forests. Bungarotoxin, a component of a poisonous snake, was isolated in Tu's laboratory by his most outstanding student, Chen-Yuan Lee. This toxin was used as a research tool to identify the site on cellular membranes where some muscle-paralysing drugs acted.

After the Japanese left Taiwan in 1945, Taipei Imperial University was renamed as the National Taiwan University. Tu was appointed as Dean of its medical college. This medical college was the only medical school in Taiwan until the Defense Medical College was refounded in Taipei in 1949, with faculties and students moved from its original campus in Shanghai. In 1954, Tu left Taiwan University to establish the first non-governmental medical school in Kaohsiung, the largest port city in southern Taiwan.

The splendid academic career of Tu included becoming the first Taiwanese promoted to a professorship, the first Taiwanese appointed as a Dean of medical school, and the first Taiwanese to found a non-governmental medical college. Tu had students all over Taiwan. Many leading medical practitioners were his former students. Inspired by Tu, my grandfather tried his best during his life to encourage his sons to develop an interest in medical research and pursue a career in academic medicine.

CHAPTER 3

The Russians Invade Manchuria. My Father Escapes in a Hurry.

To generations of Chinese people who lived in the Chinese heartland, which was the vast area south of the Great Wall, Manchuria was a foreign country. The Ancient Chinese built the Great Wall to prevent uncivilized people in the north from invading their country. To them, China was the Middle Kingdom, the centre of the world. All others were Barbarians.

In the 17th century, the Qing dynasty was founded in China by the Manchurians. The imperial court of the Qing tried their best to be as civilized as those ruled by them. Qing emperors learned to speak in Mandarin Chinese, to perfect the art of calligraphy, to sing Chinese poems, to worship the sayings of Confucius. They enjoyed all the sophisticated material and spiritual wealth of Chinese culture. The Manchurian minority was assimilated into the Chinese majority. Their status as Chinese was well recognized by themselves and by the general public. Manchuria, their homeland outside the Great Wall, became an integrated part of Chinese territory. As rulers of China, they had no objection.

In the second half of the 19th century, China became a weak country. Supported by their military forces, European superpowers started to colonize China. Japan, the newly risen power in Asia, was most interested in Manchuria, which was the part of China closest to Japan. When the Japanese defeated the Chinese in 1894, Japan asked for the annexation of a peninsula in southern Manchuria. The Qing emperor could not accept it – that strategically important peninsula was part of the sacred land from where his ancestors came. Instead, he gave Taiwan to the Japanese.

In 1900, eight foreign nations sent their troops to China to relieve the Boxers' siege of diplomatic legations in Beijing. The Boxers were a violent anti-foreign and anti-Christian militia partially supported by the Qing government. Taking this opportunity, Imperial Russia invaded Manchuria. The Russians built a railway crossing the central plain of Manchuria: both east and west ends were border stations connected to the Siberian Railway, which ran a circular route surrounding the north, west and east sides of Manchuria.

Other superpowers – Japan in particular – were not happy to see a permanent Russian occupation of Manchuria. They helped China to ask Russia to withdraw after China agreed to pay an indemnity to all eight nations.

The Russians intentionally delayed their departure. The Japanese lost patience and sent their army and navy to Manchuria in 1904. Far more Japanese soldiers died in the battle than Russian, but the former succeeded in forcing the latter to withdraw. It was the first time in history that an Eastern Asian country defeated a strong European power. In this war between two foreign countries, many Chinese people lost their lives on their own land.

Japan inherited all privileges from Russia. They created the South Manchuria Railway Company as a representative of their government in order to colonize Manchuria. Half of the shares of this company belonged to the Japanese government. They built a railway from the south to the north and monopolized all kinds of business. Many senior managers in this company were former officers in the colonial government in Taiwan. Their previous experiences in the first Japanese colony were invaluable in Manchuria.

In 1911, revolution broke out in China. This revolution led to the fall of the Qing dynasty and the establishment of the Republic of China. The six-year-old last emperor abdicated from his throne. Yet-Sen Sun, the leader of the revolution, became the first president of the republic.

Sun was one of the first two graduates in 1892 from the Hong Kong Medical College for Chinese, which was the predecessor of the Medical Faculty of the University of Hong Kong. His birthday, 12 November, was celebrated annually as the day for medical doctors in China, even though he practised medicine for only a short time.

In 1931, Chinese officers in Manchuria were expelled by the Japanese, who supported the establishment of a new State of Manchuria. The deposed last emperor of the Qing dynasty was given a new throne to sit on in the city named Hsinking, or New Capital, located at the intersection of two major railways built by the Russians and Japanese respectively. The real power of this puppet state, of course, was in the hands of the Japanese.

As in Taiwan, hygiene and health were big problems in Manchuria. Plague and other infections were spreading. The Japanese needed experts in bacteriology to work in their organization. The Taiwanese, at that time Japanese subjects, were welcome participants. My grandfather accepted an offer and brought all his family there. They sailed across the East China Sea, transited in Japan and arrived in Dalian, the seaport at the southern tip of Manchuria. From there, they took a train northward and started their new life.

Young men in Taiwan were conscripted to join the Japanese expeditionary force. Many of them died in the jungles of the southern Pacific islands. There was no such obligation to join for those in Manchuria. Protected by a strong Japanese army and away from major battlefields, the state of Manchuria was a relatively safe place during the harsh time of the Second World War.

My grandparents had five sons. The two eldest sons studied medicine at Manchuria Medical University in Shenyang, the largest city and formerly the capital for the Qing royal family in Manchuria. This university is now called China Medical University, and is still one of the leading medical universities in China.

The third and the fourth sons studied at the Hsinking Medical University in New Capital. My father was the fourth son.

The youngest son was too young to complete his medical studies in Manchuria, but he eventually got his medical degree from Taiwan University.

All five sons were qualified in medicine. This was rare at a time when most Taiwanese weren't educated beyond elementary school. Six years of primary education was compulsory in Taiwan: certainly a good policy of the colonial government.

Two days after America dropped the first atomic bomb in Hiroshima on 6 August 1945, Russia declared war on Japan. It might be surprising to know that Russia, a key member of the Allies during the Second World War, did not fight with Japan until the last moment. Owing to heavy casualties during its resistance to Germany on the European front, Russia could not afford to engage in another military action in Asia. Japan had a similar consideration, as it was stretched by combat with American, British and Chinese forces in the Pacific and Southeast Asia. Japanese generals did not want another enemy on their backs. These two rivals pretended that they were at peace throughout the most devastating years of the global war.

The Allies had persuaded the Russian leader Stalin to attack the Japanese army stationed in Manchuria in order to accelerate the unconditional surrender of Japan. The collapse of Nazi Germany in May 1945 freed up Russian forces in Europe and enabled the Soviet army to move across Siberia to concentrate at the border of Manchuria, the northeastern territory of China. Like a thunderstorm, hundreds of thousands of Russian soldiers rushed into Manchuria and controlled it immediately. A second atomic bomb left Nagasaki in ruins. The Japanese emperor ordered all his men and women to give up on 15 August 1945.

My father had just finished medical school when the Russians invaded Manchuria. He was terrified to hear the news of how Russian soldiers killed and raped. In no time, he took a southbound train and escaped from Russian-occupied Hsinking. On the way, he saw red fire in the dark sky. The Russians were burning factories after taking machines back to their country as trophies. On the train, all the women had their hair cut to avoid being noticed by the Russians. My father put his leather luggage under a dirty cover so he could pretend to be a poor traveler. All Hong family members met and stayed in Tianjin, a seaport east to Beijing. The second daughter of my grandfather had a successful business selling jewelry there. She took care of her parents and her younger brothers.

After the Japanese surrender, the name Hsinking was abandoned because of its strong political implications. The city and the medical school were renamed Changchun, or Long Spring.

Russia transferred the military equipment confiscated from the disarmed Japanese to the Communist Chinese. Soon after the end of the Second World War, a civil war broke out in China between the Nationalist government and Communist revolutionaries.

My grandparents and their children saw no future either in Manchuria or any corner of mainland China. Going back to Taiwan, the place where they were born, was the only choice they had. They boarded a ship again. For the first time, they registered their nationality as 'Republic of China'.

The eldest son of the five opened a pediatric clinic in Dalian after gaining his medical license in Manchuria. Returning to Taipei, he continued to have a successful practice and served for some years as the president of Taipei Medical Association. After retirement, he and his children emigrated to Los Angeles, California, USA. One of his daughters was a medical doctor and one son a dentist.

The second son was a surgeon. He went to the USA for clinical training and received a doctoral degree in biochemistry from Japan. His research was published in *Nature* in a paper entitled 'Substances in bone marrow extract accelerating coagulation of the blood' in 1953. Returning back to Taiwan, he became a skilful hospital administrator and served as a superintendent in several large public hospitals. He sent a son and a daughter to study medicine in Japan. They became naturalized Japanese.

The third son was a gynecologist. Unfortunately he died aged 40. His wife and children all went to the USA and stayed there permanently.

My father was the fourth son. The youngest one was a partner in the pediatric clinic of his eldest brother.

All the children of my grandparents were successful medical doctors in Taiwan, but none of them fulfilled their father's hope that they might pursue a career in academic medicine.

CHAPTER 4

A People's Republic is Established.
I am Born in the Year of Ox.

Taiwan was turbulent when my grandparents and their children returned. In 1945 when the Second World War was just over, the local Taiwanese at first gave a sincere welcome to the Chinese officers coming from the mainland. They were happy that Taiwan was reunified with the motherland after half a century of being ruled by the Japanese as a colony. However, conflict soon developed between the locals and the newcomers, or 'mainlanders' as they were called. The locals spoke in either dialect or Japanese; few of them understood these officers who talked in Mandarin Chinese. Many of the officers were as corrupt as they were on the mainland. Unemployment was everywhere and inflation out of control. People were disappointed. Life was not better. On the contrary, it got worse.

A '228 incident' erupted on 28 February, 1947. It was an anti-government uprising in Taiwan suppressed violently by military forces. The Governor-General of Taiwan was dismissed, and then executed on the charge of cooperation with the Communists. This ruling was not directly related to his mismanagement in Taiwan. The families of the dead received apologies and compensation from the government only half a century later.

In 1948, my father and mother got married. The bride was 26 and groom 19. Her maiden name was Ju-Yu, or Jade-Like in Chinese. She worked as a clerk in the Bank of Taiwan. They were introduced to each other by a matchmaker, and my mother did not take much time to accept the proposal. He was very handsome, she remembered.

Her father, Mau-Tong Chen, was one of the most successful

businessmen in Taipei. He sold Chinese herbal drugs. He was the general manager of Qian Yuan, a herbal drug shop founded in the nineteenth century, during the Qing dynasty. This shop is still open in a narrow, brick-paved street. The secrets of his success were his skill in promotion, and his capability to import herbal medicine directly from mainland China without middlemen. He was the president of an Association of Chinese Medicine which published a Journal of Chinese Medicine. Tu, professor of pharmacology at the medical school in Taipei, frequently visited him and asked him for advice about the research of medicinal herbs. He died in 1936 aged 59 when my mother was seven. My maternal grandmother remarried a few years later.

Tu, as a friend to both families of the bride and the groom, attended the wedding and gave his best wishes at the banquet.

At that time, it was clear to everyone that the Nationalist government would soon be overthrown by the Chinese Communists. The Red Army, advancing from northern China, defeated government troops in several key battles and captured the capital city, Nanjing. Kai-Shek Chiang, leader of the Nationalist Party, relocated the government to Chongqing in inland China. Chongqing was the temporal capital of China during the eight-year-long resistance to Japan between 1937 and 1945.

In August 1949, I was born at the Railway Hospital in Taipei. My grandfather was the chief of laboratory medicine there. This was a year of the Ox. Fortune-tellers would predict that babies born in such a year would have a busy life. In the Chinese zodiac, each year is represented by an animal in a 12-year cycle.

On 1 October during that same year, Ze-Dong Mao, Chairman of the Communist Party, declared from Tiananmen, which meant Gate of Heavenly Peace, that a People's Republic of China had been founded. The capital was moved to Beijing.

An aircraft evacuated Chiang to Taiwan. He had ruled China for 22 years from 1928, after he led a troop of the Nationalist Party to unify the country. He had been the leader in the war against Japan and won it. However, he lost all he had in mainland China just four years after the victory. Before he left, he ordered the transport of all gold bars belonging to the Central Bank from Shanghai to Taiwan. A huge collection of imperial treasures from the Qing Palace in Beijing was also moved to Taiwan. Now these treasures are exhibited in the Palace Museum in Taipei. More than a million of Chiang's followers came to Taiwan; most of them were soldiers or government officers loyal to him.

Martial law was imposed in Taiwan in 1949. During the following years of so-called 'White Terror' tens of thousands of people, including locals and mainlanders, were imprisoned, many of them executed. Political dissidents were prosecuted, those perceived by the government as Communists or their sympathizers were treated harshly. Meanwhile, the economy was in a parlous state. Hyperinflation was only controlled with the issue of a New Taiwanese Dollar. The exchange rate of this new dollar to the Old Taiwan Dollar was one to 40,000. At the same time, Mao's armies in mainland China were preparing to attack this island. It was a dark time in Taiwan when I was born.

My father kept a distance from politics and worked in the Hygienic Laboratory of Taiwan Provincial Government. Most likely he was encouraged by his father. There were few places for medical research, except in the medical college of National Taiwan University. The Hygienic Laboratory was an alternative for my father if he wanted to do medical research. When he was off duty from his official job, he saw patients in a small clinic. At that time, medical doctors employed in governmental institutions were allowed to keep certain hours for private practice to supplement their salary.

He was promoted to being Section Chief in Bacteriology and Serology. He focused his research on newly developed serological testing for syphilis and published a series of papers. When the Provincial Government opened a Venereal Disease Control Centre, he was assigned to participate in this project. Consultants from the World Health Organization came to this centre. He worked with them in epidemiological survey, case-finding, patient treatment and public education. He taught students at Taiwan University College of Public Health about venereal disease. When a Taiwanese team of medical delegates made the first official visit to Japan after Taiwan returned to China, he was a member of that team. President Chiang received them in his office before these delegates left for Japan.

He had a talent for languages. He spoke fluent Japanese, Mandarin Chinese and Taiwanese dialect. His second language in medical school was German, as it was for most Japanese university students before the end of the Second World War. When learning English became a necessity for any young men ambitious to have a brighter future, he studied English and studied it very hard. His efforts were well rewarded. The United States International Cooperation Administration (later called US Agency for International Development) gave him a one year fellowship to Johns Hopkins University at Baltimore, Maryland, to study public health administration.

He left Taiwan in 1956. In addition to a master's degree in Public Health, he got a diploma in venereal disease control. His training in the latter was made under Professor Joseph Moore at Johns Hopkins Hospital. He kept a friendship with the Moores, and exchanged Christmas cards with the professor's wife after her husband died, until she also passed away. Moore Clinic was once a centre for chronic disease; now it is the centre for HIV infection at Johns Hopkins. HIV as a venereal disease was never known to Moore's generation.

Returning to Taiwan, he served in the Provincial Government until all its offices were moved to central Taiwan. This move was intended to separate the function of the central government in Taipei from that of the provincial one. The provincial level of government was eventually abolished, making the management structure more streamlined and efficient.

After leaving governmental service my father became a full-time practitioner and examined patients every weekday in our house. The front rooms were refurbished to make a clinic with an office, a small pharmacy and a patient waiting area. My mother helped him sometimes in the clinic, although she had no medical training at all.

My father did not allow me to stay in the clinic if patients were present. When no one was there, I could touch his instruments and scan his books. Unable to read in English, I was curious about the illustrations.

I have a sister, Mei-Chen Hong, who is three years younger than me, active and extrovert. I do not remember that my father ever spent time in supervising our study at home. However, he did encourage us to read extensively. He subscribed us to a daily newspaper for kids and a monthly journal for children. Father rarely went out for social gatherings. We had dinner together every evening. He talked with us, telling stories about medicine, current or ancient. He commented on the work of other medical doctors, and advised us to follow those he respected. It was obvious that he wished me to take up the family tradition of studying medicine, but I was not sure if I liked it.

City University of Osaka, Japan granted him a doctoral degree after he submitted an application and sent all his publications as references. Of the five sons of his father, he put the greatest effort into medical research. But like others, he ended up in clinical practice. That was not a bad job. He was well-respected and admired. He supported his family well. However, I knew that he was not satisfied, because he did not become a research-oriented academic physician as his father expected. In this house of Hong, medical research was the ultimate virtue.

CHAPTER 5

America Defends Taiwan.
Respectable Teachers Guide Young Men.

I n 1950, the North Korean army crossed the 38th parallel north, which divided Korea into a Communist north and an American-supported south. This Korean War strengthened American determination to block the expansion of Communism in East Asia.

Taiwan became one of America's strongest allies. The China White Paper, which criticized President Chiang and his Nationalist Party, issued by the US Department of States in 1949, was put aside. An American Military Assistance Advisory Group came to Taiwan to provide military advice and equipment and to assist with military training. Under a Taiwan Defense Commander, America set up military bases in Taiwan, mostly for its air forces.

On a Saturday afternoon in 1957, two third-year elementary-school students in Taipei were hit by a car driven by the wife of an American military officer. One of the boys suffered only a light injury; the other one lost consciousness. The latter was sent to nearby Mackay Memorial Hospital where he awoke six hours later. His clavicle bone was found to be broken. The boy with a minor bruise was Ing-Sh Chiu, who later became professor of cardiovascular surgery at Taiwan University. The boy who lost consciousness was me. We two were classmates, returning home together from a painting lesson. This accident happened in front of the main gate of the residence for the Commander of American Military Assistance Advisory Group in Taiwan. This mansion with a beautiful garden was not far from my home.

Mackay Memorial Hospital, where I was hospitalized, was named in memory of George Mackay, a Canadian Presbyterian missionary. In 1880, he set up a Mackay Clinic in Tamsui, a suburb of Taipei. That clinic was named in honor of Captain Mackay, whose wife donated a fund to support it. In 1912, a new hospital was built in downtown Taipei; by that time George Mackay had passed away. Mackay Memorial Hospital is now one of the busiest medical centres in Taipei, with a new Mackay Medical College affiliated to it. Christians, Presbyterians in particular, built several hospitals in Taiwan. Some of these hospitals developed into large medical centres, such as Mackay.

Zhongshan Elementary School, where I studied, was also the school my mother attended. I was not a brilliant student when I started. However, after the traffic accident and my six-hour loss of consciousness, I showed an obvious improvement in my study. Wen-Dau Zhuang, a fresh graduate, was assigned to be the leading teacher of our class. He liked to ask students questions – quite different from conventional Taiwanese teachers who only pushed students to memorize what they had been taught. He noticed that I was always the first, or the only one, to answer his questions. He recommended that I participate in oratory contests and take leading roles in student plays, and he chose me to get the Mayor's Award when I graduated. This award was given to the best student in the class. Wen-Dau Zhuang was the teacher who gave me confidence and opportunities; my first mentor, a man I should sincerely thank and respect all my life. He lived in Los Angeles with his children after he retired. I was privileged to take care of his health when he came back to Taiwan for vacation.

I passed an examination and entered Datong Junior High School, my first choice school. All male students were required to have their hair cut like soldiers and wear a uniform like that of boy scouts.

The leading teacher for my class during my three years in junior high school served in the marine corps before teaching us. He strongly emphasized the importance of physical health, asking us to do exercise before and after classes. It was not required by the school. Still single, he had plenty of time to spend with us taking part in various sports. At weekends, our class bicycled to the countryside where we swam in the river and camped overnight. Friendship among classmates was so strong that we still gathered 50 years later. I was in no way a sports fan, but I appreciated very much that he trained my body to be fit and strong during my teenage years.

Der-Hai Hsiao, one of my best friends, was my classmate in both junior and senior high school. He attended school late, so he was three years older than most classmates. Nicknamed 'old man', he was modest, sincere, and always willing to help everyone, like an elder brother. He later became an ophthalmologist. We were planning to travel around the world together after we retired; unfortunately he died of a stroke before we could achieve our plan.

Aged 15, I was admitted to the Chien-Kou Senior High School. Founded by the Japanese as the First High School in Taipei, it enjoyed a reputation as the best high school in Taiwan.

Unlike many other high schools – which asked their students to stay inside the campus all day – students at this relatively liberal school were allowed to spend their lunch break outside school.

Opposite the main gate was a beautiful botanic garden containing a national library, a science museum and a history museum. The US Information Service was also in the neighborhood; its library and galleries were open to the public. There I had my first experience of an open-shelf library; there were no restrictions on access to reading material. The rich collection of American books and journals broadened the minds of young Taiwanese. Many of us chose to study, work or live in the USA after finishing our universities in Taiwan. The library was a very good shop-window for American culture when the USA was the leader of the democratic world. Only after a long time did I realize that America had many dark sides, as does any part of the world.

Many teachers in this prestigious high school were graduates from leading universities in mainland China. They came with the Nationalist government to Taiwan in the 1940s. I was most impressed by our teachers in Chinese, history and other humanistic courses. They taught us how to enjoy classic Chinese poems and other literary masterpieces. Their influences on me were everlasting: I developed a lifelong interest in these subjects.

During summer and winter vacations, I often took part in activities such as hiking, camping, or study groups in art and history organized by the China Youth National Salvation Corps. This was a quasi-governmental organization with close ties to the dominating Nationalist Party, similar in many ways to the Communist Youth League in Red China. In these recreational activities, politics was minimized to the extent that it was almost non-existent in order to show care and kindness to young students. For us, the most attractive part of these activities was the female students from girls' schools. In most high schools, male and female students were segregated, but on these occasions, we could mix for a week. We were away from our parents, living in different dorms but eating, learning and traveling together. Teenagers at that time in Taiwan were ultra-conservative, unlike our counterparts in America and Europe during the 'hippy' years. Even limited body contact was avoided, unless it was unintentional. A kiss was an equivalent to engagement; living together was unthinkable. A playboy was risking his future career.

Students at senior high schools were divided into several groups depending on their choice of career. Subjects for University Entrance Examination varied. In addition to common requirements such as Chinese, English, politics and mathematics, those who chose to be an engineer or scientist had to take examinations in physics and chemistry. History and geography were required for literature, law and social science studies, while biology and chemistry were needed for medical and agricultural studies.

I was considering choosing law as my future profession, based on my interest and academic performance. I did best in humanities courses in high school and this was compatible with my choice. But when I started to discuss this with my father, he said without a second thought: 'Go to the medical school.' He then told me that he intended to become a lawyer when he was young, but his father rejected his idea and asked him to study medicine first, before shifting to any other career. He promised me that he would let me do whatever I liked if I completed medical school. My mother was more sympathetic. 'Being the wife of a medical doctor, I know how hard a doctor's life is, but you better listen to your father,' she said to me. I followed my father's orders, not wanting to offend him.

My scores in the University Entrance Examination were not high enough for me to enter my first choice, Taiwan University Medical College. I was accepted by my second choice, Taipei Medical College. I was not sure I could complete the seven-year course there, not to mention enjoy it.

PART TWO

*Learning Medicine from Books
and Patients*

CHAPTER 6

Military Training.
Learning Basic Medical Courses.

I enrolled as a first-year medical student in the summer of 1967. A 10-year-long culture revolution in China just started while the Vietnam War (which lasted from 1955-1975) was at its peak. Taiwan maintained a strong military force of half a million soldiers by drafting every young man into the army for a minimum of two years.

Male university students were required to receive two months' military training before starting their freshman year. My father accompanied me on the train to a military base in central Taiwan. With the exception of some short trips outside Taipei with friends, I had never left home. My father worried that this 18-year-old boy could adjust to a life without parental protection. The army base on Chenggongling, or Ridge of Success, is a common memory for a million Taiwanese men, who experienced there the transformation from civilian to soldier.

The first thing was to have our hair shaved in the style of a monk. It was the training sergeants' job to keep us alert every minute and push our tolerance to the extreme. A 'combat bath' involved pouring cold water over new recruits from head to foot and changing clothes before and after – in a total of three minutes. Physical training involved running 3,000 meters under hot summer sun. 'Marching' was carrying nearly 20kg, including a rifle, on your back and walking on an endless sandy road with no sign of shadow. A sharp whistle awakened 100 tired comrades sleeping together on a long wooden double-deck bed at night. Punishment awaited those who were slow. Rice was half-cooked, with tiny stones in it; but we all ate it very fast.

There were interesting parts to military training, of course. Everyone was given a rifle and asked to treat it as his second life. We learned to separate it into parts and tenderly clean the cold steel every day. Very few Taiwanese were allowed to own a weapon; a rifle with a bayonet attached was certainly a big toy. Shooting exercises with real bullets were most exciting. We were once put into an airtight chamber to experience tear gas. We were not allowed to put on face masks until our eyes and noses were so irritated that tears and water were running over our faces. We were shown, and allowed to touch, heavy equipment such as machine guns, cannons, armored vehicles and tanks. We sang marching songs loudly together to show our solidarity. When movie stars came to the barracks to entertain us, we all shouted like crazy.

With tanned skin and newly grown hair, we entered the gate of Taipei Medical College. It was located in a newly developed area in eastern Taipei. On my hour-long bus ride from home to school, I could still see farmhouses scattered in rice fields. Among 125 classmates, only one girl drove a car. She was unusual, even among medical students who mostly came from middle-class families. Twenty-five of my classmates were overseas Chinese. They had attended high schools in Hong Kong, Macau, Malaysia, Thailand or Japan and came to Taiwan for medical education.

Less than 10% of our classmates were female. They were looked after very well not only by those in the same classroom, but also by senior students on campus, and were invited to many parties.

There were six medical schools in Taiwan in the 1960s; they were National Taiwan University Medical College, National Defense Medical College and four non-governmental ones: one in Taipei, two in Taichung, central Taiwan, and one in Kaohsiung in the south.

Forty years after I graduated from the medical school, the number of medical schools had increased from six to 13. Every year, around 1,500 new medical doctors graduated to serve a population of 23 million. Of the seven medical schools opened after the 1960s, two were founded by the government, National Yang-Ming in Taipei and National Cheng-Kung in Tainan, southern Taiwan. Three were founded by religious organizations and the other two by business groups. There was one Buddhist, one Christian and one Catholic medical school. In medical schools founded by religious organizations, there is no restriction on the religion of the students, and no religious courses were compulsory in any of them.

Tuition for non-governmental medical schools in 2014 was around US$5,000 a year, twice as much as governmental ones. Defense Medical College was a military school, students did not have to pay anything; on the other hand, they were given a salary, but they were obliged to serve as military medical officers for a number of years after graduation.

In 1960, a group of prominent medical doctors worked together to establish Taipei Medical College. There were five schools in the college, namely medicine, dentistry, pharmacy, nursing and medical technology. The latter two were vocational in nature; junior high graduates were admitted for a five-year course. Senior high school graduates got their university degree in the medical, dental or pharmacy schools after seven, six or four years of study respectively.

All Taiwanese medical schools taught modern Western medicine. In the 1960s, only China Medical College in Taichung provided a separate school to teach traditional Chinese medicine. Students here studied both Western and Chinese medicine, so they were allowed to get a license to practice modern medicine if they passed an examination. However, one could only practice one type of medicine even if one held two licenses, because Western and Chinese medicine were regulated by different laws. Most graduates chose to be modern rather than traditional.

A typical seven-year medical curriculum included two years each in pre-medical, basic and clinical courses plus a one-year internship.

Honestly speaking, I did not make much effort with my studies during the pre-medical years. Most of the courses were duplicates of those I had taken in senior high school. The only difference was that the textbooks and lecture notes were all in English. Lectures were given in Chinese, but we had to learn every science term in English so we could read English medical books and papers in our future career.

I took part in various extra-curricular activities, including becoming president of a debate club and editor of several student journals. I wrote commentary articles using my real name and romantic poems under a pen name, Rainbow Mountain. Like moaning without being ill, as far as I remember, these poems were not dedicated to any specific girl.

Once, after camping on a beach, I suffered from hepatitis. My skin, eyelids and urine all turned a deep yellow. I was weak and badly nauseated. Lying on my bed at home for a whole week, my fluids and nutrients were supplied through intravenous infusion. My father treated me and my mother prepared hot clam-and-ginger soup for me when my appetite had improved. Clam-and-ginger soup was a Taiwanese folk remedy for jaundice. Ironically, contaminated shellfish was thought to be a source of orally transmitted infectious hepatitis.

A classmate visited me at my bedside. He advised me to read Shakespeare's plays, in Chinese of course. This was the start of my lifelong admiration for this English genius. Owing to my long sick leave, I failed to pass the year-end tests for organic chemistry and analytical chemistry, two courses in which I had little interest. My professors kindly let me have a second try.

Real medical courses started with anatomy. Dissection of a cadaver was unforgettable for any medical student. It was on the anatomy table I realized that I could never be a good surgeon, or any type of medical doctor requiring a skilful hand. Blood vessels, muscle tendons and nerves all became mixed up under my knife, while one of my classmates separated them beautifully. That classmate later became a neurosurgeon.

Osteology, or study of the bones, was a special part of anatomy. Students were divided into several groups, each one given a complete skeleton. The skull was the most complicated part, with its many tiny components and curving canals. Everyone in the group liked to spend more time studying the skull; however, they had to share it.

An open secret among medical students was the transfer of a skull of unknown origin from a senior student to his favorite junior. The skull was invaluable in the study of anatomy so whoever received the gift would appreciate it and never want to trace the source. I got one and put it in the closet of my bedroom, carefully studying it at night. Once my father discovered it, he was indifferent. He might have had one when he was younger.

Other courses during the basic medicine years included physiology (the study of body function), biochemistry (chemistry within the body), pathology (the cause and effects of diseases), immunology (resistance within the body), microbiology (the study of pathogenic bacteria, virus and parasites) and pharmacology (the study of drugs).

Immunology was badly taught; I wonder if the instructor really had sufficient knowledge. I had difficulty remembering the bizarre names and detailed characteristics of microorganisms; my grandfather's and father's talent in microbiology was not transmitted to me. Physiology and biochemistry were fine. I liked to observe pathological specimens under the microscope; they were colorful and fascinating, even though they were body tissues damaged by fatal diseases. Professor of pathology, Ding-Yao Chen, was a cousin of my father. Chen was regarded by most students as the best teacher in the campus; his teaching was always concise, clear and in good order. He played American football, but I never had the courage to take part.

I had a special interest in pharmacology, even though the lectures were poorly given. Most classmates were fed up being forced to memorize the names of drugs. I however, tried my best to check all the details in the pharmacology textbook. If I could not be a surgeon because of my poor manual skills, an internist would be my best choice and drugs would be my main tool for treating patients.

The workload was heavy. Many of my classmates developed a syndrome common to all medical students: finding an abnormality in the body and self-diagnosing a serious disease described in the textbook. I accidentally discovered a peanut-sized lymph node in my neck. My worry was alleviated only after a specialist doctor assured me it was neither tuberculosis nor malignant lymphoma. Sometimes, however, knowledge did relieve anxiety. One classmate told us that he had been worried for years since he noticed his right testis was higher than the left – anatomy class taught him to realize it was perfectly normal.

CHAPTER 7

First Encounter with Patients.
I Fall in Love with Fumi.

The chief resident of surgery was making his afternoon rounds in the ward, followed by a few medical students and a nurse who pushed a cart. It was the first day on rotation in the surgical ward for me and my classmates in the same team. A chief resident was the highest level of medical doctors still being trained in a hospital. He would soon be promoted to attending doctor; he was often assigned to give bedside teaching to medical students.

We walked to a young man, his right arm covered with a white bandage. The chief resident told us this patient was burned and he would like to change the dressing; routine work. I noticed the man was anxious.

The bandage was removed layer by layer. Blood and yellowish oozing tinted the deeper layers. When all the cotton gauze was removed we saw a large wound. A mesh covered its centre. The chief resident moistened the wound with wet cotton balls and told the patient, 'just a few seconds, endure for a while'. He then used a tweezer to remove the mesh stuck to the wound. It was so tight that he had to pull forcefully. I could see the patient was in great pain; he closed his eyes tight, bit his teeth and stretched all his extremities. It was certain that he had experienced this pain before.

I felt dizzy and my chest tightened; I could not stand. Immediately I left the room and went outside, taking deep breaths. Sitting on a chair in the corridor, I assured myself again I did not want to be a surgeon.

Pain control was not a priority to most medical doctors when I was a medical student. Professors never taught us that patients were entitled to have pain-free treatment. What they showed to us was an indifference to the patients' feelings. Authority over patients, rather than empathy for them, was the attitude of most senior doctors. Thinking back today, I regretted that education about the doctor-patient relationship in most Taiwanese medical schools was misleading to students of my generation. It took us many years to realize that we needed a change.

Fifth and sixth year medical students were divided into several groups. Since the Taipei Medical College Hospital was yet to be opened, each group was assigned in rotation to different clinical departments at several large hospitals in Taipei. Many senior doctors in these hospitals were appointed as adjunct faculty members of the medical college; they had responsibility to teach students rotated to their departments.

Students spent each morning in these hospitals. We were mostly observers, watching how hospital staff handled patients in the ambulatory clinic, emergency room, medical ward or surgical theater. In the afternoon, we returned to campus and attended lectures on various disciplines of clinical medicine, such as internal medicine, surgery, pediatrics, obstetrics and gynecology etc.

One day, I was sitting in a delivery room. A pregnant woman in a gown was lying on the table and nurses were preparing the instruments. She could have a baby at any time; we were all waiting for that moment. She was impatient; while the nurses were away for a while, she turned her body, climbed down from the table and started to walk around the room. I did not know what I should do. After all, I was a naïve student without any experience.

Suddenly, we heard a loud flushing sound like water pouring to the ground; fluid was flowing from between her legs to the floor. Her amniotic membrane had ruptured. A nurse rushed to the room to help her back to the table. An obstetrician and a pediatrician arrived to start the delivery procedure. I watched: for the first time in my life I saw a baby being born. The woman was fortunate that her baby did not fall out of her along with the amniotic fluid.

The president of Taipei Medical College was Professor Chien-Tien Hsu, a prominent gynecologist most famous for his operations on cervical cancer. Before routine Papanicolaou smear was used as a screening and prevention method, cervical cancer was the most common and lethal cancer for Taiwanese women. It is now becoming less common, unlike breast cancer. Many students at our medical college made obstetrics/gynecology their priority when selecting a specialty for their future practice, mainly inspired by the successful story of Hsu. I did not think I could enjoy a life in which I was awakened at night to deliver babies, so I did not consider that option.

Professor of pediatrics Sou-Tien Lin was one of the few clinical teachers who left a deep impression on me. He trained at the Great Ormond Street Hospital for Sick Children in London. Specializing in blood diseases including childhood leukemia, he was not only a gentle and patient doctor but also an enthusiastic and skilful teacher. Many years later, we became colleagues; he wrote recommendation letters for me when I was applying for a training position in England. I had difficulty communicating with kids, and felt helpless when they were crying. Pediatrics did not fit with me. Long after my student years, I realized that pediatricians communicated mostly with the mothers, not the children.

Since we had no duty to serve the patients and most professors in clinical medicine were busy with their clinical practice, life during these two clinical years was much easier than the previous two, learning basic medical courses.

In the fifth year at medical school, I was editor-in-chief of the student journal. I radically changed the format as well as the style of the journal. After this change, it was awarded the best university student journal in Taiwan. Many students who volunteered to participate in editorial work shared common interests. I made lifelong friendships with several of them. When I became an academic administrator during the later stages of my career, we were able to work together and help each other again.

The whole world was surprised to know that Nixon, the strongly anti-Communist American president, visited China and met with Ze-Dong Mao in 1972. Associated with this political event was a sudden American interest in acupuncture, shown to them by Chinese doctors. American medical delegates were amazed to see patients who had received acupuncture undergoing major operation without anesthesia.

Traditional Chinese medicine was not taught in our medical school. Students interested in acupuncture organized a study club and invited practising acupuncturists to teach this skill. I was one of the members of this club.

When I was preparing a paper on the theory of acupuncture for publication in the student journal, I asked Fu-Mei Wang, a pharmacy student, to help me prepare the illustrations. Fumi was also a member of the club, she was two years my junior.

I had first met Fumi three years previously during the welcome party for freshmen. That party was jointly organized by alumni of my Chien-Kou Senior High School and Taipei First Girls Senior High School. They were the best high schools for male and female students in Taipei respectively. On that occasion, I was caught when I first saw her, a petite girl with bright eyes and a shy smile. The workload of my basic medical courses prevented me from spending time on anything other than the textbooks. Before we learned acupuncture together, we exchanged hellos with each other when we met on campus.

We were asked by the teacher to insert acupuncture needles to specific points on the hands and legs of students sitting next to us. I volunteered to let her try on the Zu-San-Li point of my leg: this point was said to regulate digestive function. She did not let me try on her in return, but we started to talk and I asked her for help with illustrations.

She gave me 14 hand-drawn cartoons, each one representing an acupuncture meridian. After school, we walked together to the bus station. We had talked endlessly. In less than one week, I was in love, hot and fierce love. After the first kiss of my life, by a lakeside, I promised her I would marry her.

I had long been known as a young man with a strong passion and my father was always worried about my hasty decisions. I informed my parents of my decision to marry Fumi without even introducing her to them. My father was upset and asked me to cool down. Although relatively open-minded among Taiwanese parents because of his experience abroad, he could not be forced to accept a future daughter-in-law without prior consultation. I insisted on continuing the relationship and tried to find all possibly opportunities to meet Fumi. She stood firmly beside me, never suggesting a separation because of the objections of my father.

In Taiwan, professors recommended English textbooks to us and considered Chinese ones inferior in quality. In reality, most students never used English books because it was time-consuming to read them. They ended up reading lecture-notes only in order to pass the examinations.

A group of young doctors at Taiwan University Hospital made a huge effort to translate the complete volume of *Harrison's Principles of Internal Medicine* into Chinese in 1972, when I was a fifth-year medical student just starting my clinical courses. Professor Juei-Low Sung, chief of internal medicine at Taiwan University Medical College, was a consultant on this translated book. Some of the translators later took leading medical positions in Taiwan. For example, Bor-Shen Hsieh became Dean of his medical college while Yun-Fan Liaw was elected as a member at Academia Sinica for his outstanding research in hepatitis.

On the day I got my copy of *Harrison's Principles of Internal Medicine*, I carried it to a bench near the campus tennis court. It was late afternoon; I just wanted to have a quick look at the book while waiting for Fumi.

Immediately the first paragraph of the first chapter moved me.

'No greater opportunity or obligation can fall the lot of a human being than to be a physician. –. He will build an enduring edifice of character within himself. The physician should ask of his destiny no more than this and he should be content with no less'.

At that moment I suddenly realized that a career in internal medicine was my destiny. The road ahead was clear to me; there was no need for me to search for something greater.

Over the following two years, I read the 2,136-page book from cover to cover. Checking the Chinese translation against the English original, I picked up 735 items that required a revision and sent a list of them to the translators.

My knowledge of internal medicine was very much enriched. But reading a textbook is not enough to become a good doctor, as Osler once said:

'He who studies medicine without books sails an unchartered sea, but he who studies medicine without patients is not going to sea at all'.

Medical students' 'internship' was our training with patients; I completed my internship at Tri-Service General Hospital in Taipei.

CHAPTER 8

An Intern Commits Suicide.
The President and My Father Pass Away.

I was examining the urine specimen of a patient in the small laboratory of a medical ward at Tri-Service General Hospital. A fellow intern ran to tell me that another classmate of ours had committed suicide. I was the head intern among 30 coming from Taipei Medical College in this hospital.

Seventh-year medical students spent all their time in hospital. This year of internship was their first experience as a full-time member of medical staff. The most senior students in the school became the lowest level of medical doctor in the hospital. Interns' main jobs were routine, such as writing medical histories, examining blood, stools and urine, changing dressings, setting intravenous injection routes, checking laboratory reports, transporting patients to the operation rooms and getting X-ray films from radiology. By taking part in these activities, they learned the art of medicine. Internship was the best way to learn by doing.

Tri-Service General Hospital, the largest military hospital in Taiwan, was the major teaching hospital for Defense Medical College. Interns from other medical colleges also served here. It was a busy hospital, famous for its emphasis on discipline. All staff, except interns like us, possessed certain military ranks, so they had to obey orders from their superiors. Absolute obedience to orders was a unique characteristic of this hospital; some interns from civilian medical colleges had difficulty getting used to it.

That classmate was treated in the emergency room where he received a life-saving blood transfusion. He had not shown up for work that morning.

A curious colleague opened the door of his bedroom and found him unconscious. He had cut the artery in his wrist; blanket and floor were all stained with blood.

Depression was common among medical students, not only in military hospitals. Medical doctors were high suicide risks. In addition to suicide, there were drug addicts and alcoholics among medical professionals, partly because they had easy access to drugs.

The intern could have been sent home and treated with antidepressants. It would take weeks or months for the drugs to work so his internship would be delayed. An alternative was to give him electric-shock therapy. His parents could not make the decision. I advised them to choose the shock therapy suggested by the psychiatrist. I watched him cramped like an epileptic patient while an electric current passed between two sides of his head. He recovered smoothly, not only from the blood loss, but also from depression.

After medical school, he went to the United States where he became a board certified pathologist. He then returned to Taiwan to serve in a local hospital. For reasons unknown to me, he attempted suicide again; this time he succeeded.

In the 1974 commencement ceremony at Taipei Medical College, I gave a speech on behalf of all graduates. Traditionally, only thanks to teachers were delivered. However, I criticized the board of directors and school administrators for failing to build a teaching hospital on campus. I made the occasion awkward for them, but my classmates applauded for a long time.

Coming out from Taipei Medical College, I became a fully licensed medical doctor. Government regulations required me to serve in the army as a medical officer first.

All male medical graduates of the same year gathered in a small military base in suburban Taipei to receive a short period of training in military medicine. On the last day of training, each one picked a small piece of paper from a black box. He would then report to the unit whose name was printed on the paper.

Lucky ones went to hospitals where they would work like ordinary medical doctors. An assignment close to one's home was not bad, at least the doctor could go home and meet his girlfriend (if he had one) when he was off duty.

Less lucky ones were sent to Kinmen or Matsu. These two tiny islands were located off the coast of Fukien province in China. All islands were under the threat of bombardment from the other side of a narrow waterway. In some parts of the island, activities of Communist soldiers a few thousand meters away could be observed through a telescope. In 1958, Communist Chinese tried to block supplies to Kinmen from Taiwan. During the heavy bombing that lasted for months, many soldiers and civilians died, including three deputy defense commanders. A total of 470,000 artillery shells fell into this 150-square-kilometer island. It was extremely difficult for those dispatched to these islands to find a few days to come back to Taiwan for vacation.

I served in the 68th army division stationed in Yang-Mei, a small town 50 kilometers south of Taipei. This division had just moved back from its two years' rotation in Matsu, so in the coming two years it would not be leaving Taiwan unless in an emergency.

The barracks were built on the top of a hill. I worked in the medical battalion as a second lieutenant. This battalion opened a small clinic to serve everyone in the division, from the general to the private. There were rooms for examination, minor operations, and observation. There was also a pharmacy and a dental chair and among the medical officers there was a dentist and a pharmacist. Skin infection, abdominal pain, diarrhea and flu were the most common ailments. We were often asked by the boy-faced soldiers to inject penicillin for the treatment of their urethritis. We repaired minor wounds and gave fluid to soldiers who collapsed in hot summer. Sometimes one of my colleagues would perform a circumcision if he was asked to; he was preparing his future career as a surgeon. Severe cases were transferred to large military hospitals.

We also had to take part in training and exercises. As an officer, I was given a pistol, not a rifle. During a large-scale military exercise that lasted for several days, I was on board the ambulance painted with a red-cross sign meandering through the hills of northern Taiwan. A bomb blasted by accident. A private was killed. I was asked to examine his body and sign the death certificate in the morgue of a local hospital. He had a deep, penetrating wound in his chest.

Weapons were easily accessible so arms discipline was strictly enforced. A private killed his senior during a quarrel. He was soon sentenced to death. All soldiers were required to watch the public execution. He knelt, eyes blindfolded. When the bullet was shot into his heart from the back, he leaned forward immediately. It was the only time in my life I saw how a man was killed. I was not asked to sign his death certificate.

During free time in the barracks, I read in English the 18th edition of *The Principle and Practice of Medicine*. This classic medical textbook was first published in 1892 by William Osler. Osler was born in Canada and received his medical education at McGill University in Montreal. He served as a professor of medicine, first at the University of Pennsylvania in Philadelphia, then at Johns Hopkins in Baltimore, and finally in Oxford where he was a Regius Professor. Not only an outstanding clinician, he was a top-notch researcher, productive writer, and above all, a great educator.

My father brought back from America some books on Johns Hopkins Medical Institutions. The legend of Osler and his colleagues there fascinated me. I wrote a mini-review on the impact of Johns Hopkins on American medical education. This paper, entitled *Good Doctor, Good Teacher* was published in a student journal when I was 22 years old. In this paper, I highlighted Osler's contribution to clinical education. Osler was my role model, even though he died half a century before I started to learn medicine.

I tore apart the textbook into several sections, carrying only one with me so I could read it whenever it was convenient. I checked the English pronunciation of each medical term and read it loudly, if nobody was nearby. Most of the English pronunciations of my Japanese-educated professors were inaccurate.

A few months after I started in the army, my father began to suffer a yellowish discoloration of his skin. He was admitted to Taiwan University Hospital. At that time, there was no ultrasound, computerized tomography or endoscopy; otherwise his disease could have been quickly and accurately diagnosed. He was treated as if he had liver cirrhosis. Worried that his symptoms might be worsened, his physician did not recommend exploratory abdominal surgery to see if his bile duct was obstructed. His health deteriorated day by day. He lost weight because he could not eat well. Fluid accumulated in his abdomen and his leg was edematous. He also had gastrointestinal bleeding.

Repeated hospitalization only resulted in temporary relief of his symptoms. Virus testing was not yet available to pinpoint the cause of his liver abnormality. Retrospectively, the most likely cause was an accidental piercing of his finger by a needle contaminated with the blood of a patient.

He had several episodes of such an injury; many of his patients were at high risk of hepatitis.

My sister Mei-Chen had just graduated from the school of pharmacy at Taiwan University. Her boyfriend Tien-Chun Chang was an intern at the hospital. They took great care of my father. Fumi and my sister took turns accompanying my father when he was hospitalized. I could only visit him when I came back from the barracks to Taipei at weekends. My father, who a few years previously had rejected my proposal to marry Fumi, became very close to her and had many long talks with her when I was not present.

On 5 April 1975, there was a sudden thunderstorm at midnight. I was awakened, as were many others. In the morning, all soldiers were called to gather in the central court of the barrack. We heard the shocking news of the death of President Kai-Shek Chiang. Every year, 5 April was the traditional festival in which Chinese would go to the tombs of their ancestors, clean them and burn incense in front of the tombstone.

At age 87, Chiang's death should not have been surprising. But we were not prepared for the news because his health had been kept top secret. All soldiers were put into full alert so we could respond immediately if the Chinese army from the mainland attacked Taiwan. Nobody was allowed to leave the barracks, no matter how important his personal business was. Until the president's funeral was over, I did not have much chance to see my father.

By early June, my father had deteriorated into such a critical condition that his physician told us his life could only be counted in days. We were prepared for the worst.

One day before his death, my father held Fumi's hand and asked her to marry me. He knew his son could never find a better wife. Two families arranged a traditional engagement ceremony the next morning. We returned to the hospital in the afternoon; he had a very low blood pressure, but he was still able to give us his last blessing. He told Fumi never to be afraid, and passed away at four o'clock.

Three nuns sang Buddhist sutras besides his body. Fumi and I knelt and cried. Only the hymn of the sutra could slightly relieve my sorrow.

Tien-Chun Chang was very helpful to us during the difficult time. My sister married him two years later. He became a professor of medicine at Taiwan University. Widely respected in Taiwan as the best endocrinologist specializing in thyroid disorders, he was a productive writer and tireless editor. Since 1994, he has been editing a textbook on internal medicine. With its sixth edition numbering 1,822 pages, it was the most comprehensive medical textbook written in Chinese, rather than translated. Even though he was extremely busy, he still found time to paint and play the saxophone.

CHAPTER 9

Residency in Internal Medicine. USA Severs its Formal Ties with Taiwan.

Soon after my discharge from the army, Fumi and I got married. We spent the first night of our honeymoon at the Han-Bi-Lo Hotel on Sun Moon Lake in central Taiwan. This hotel was one of President Kai-Shek Chiang's favorite places to spend his summer vacation. Chiang believed in Feng-Shui, or wind and water theory of ancient China. In order to harmonize his physical presence with his environment, all his rooms and furniture were perfectly located and facing in certain directions. From a Feng-Shui point of view, the hotel sits on the most favorable site.

The morning view of the lake and mountain from Han-Bi-Lo is one of the most beautiful scenes in the world. I might be biased saying so, but I did enjoy the picturesque surroundings. This hotel has been refurbished and named Lalu and is now the most luxurious resort hotel in Taiwan. Lalu is the name of a small island at the junction of the sun-shaped half and the moon-shaped half of the lake.

Taiwan is a beautiful island; no wonder it was called Ilha Formosa by the Portuguese sailors who passed by several centuries ago. Although of similar size and population to the Netherlands, Taiwan is not flat but hilly in most parts. Jade Mountain in central Taiwan is 3,952 meters high. Within one hour's drive of Taipei, visitors can enjoy both hiking in mountains of 1,000 meters and watersports in long beaches along the coast.

Taipei Medical College Hospital opened in August 1976. It was relatively small for a teaching hospital. I was one of its first residents. A resident is a medical doctor receiving training in a specialty, such as medicine, surgery, obstetrics/gynecology or pediatrics. Residents are responsible for the care of most inpatients, under the supervision of attending physicians. Residents stay overnight at the hospital in rotation so they can answer the call of patients at night – this is why they are called residents. In England, this level of doctor is called registrar.

While I chose the newly opened hospital of my alma mater medical school for my residency, most of my classmates went to more established hospitals because they wondered whether a young doctor could receive adequate training in a new, small hospital.

Fortunately, several senior doctors joined this new hospital with a vision that someday it would be developed into a centre of excellence, not only in clinical service, but also in teaching and research. I shared this idealism.

Unlike many big Taiwanese hospitals where medical doctors were overloaded with clinical duties, our senior doctors could spend more time teaching the juniors. We followed one of Osler's mottoes: 'The value of experience is not in seeing many, but in seeing wisely'. Every case was carefully studied and discussed in great detail.

The chief of internal medicine was one of the founders of Taipei Medical College; he sat on the board of directors. Being older, he spent most of his time in his own clinic. Deputy Chief Chien-An Lai was an alumnus nine years my senior; he had just returned from the United States where he had completed his training in hematology, or blood diseases. He was always pleasant and very knowledgeable.

Chung-Ze Liu, also Lai's age, was a cardiologist. Every week, he assigned me a newly published paper to read and gave me his comments during our discussion. That I could read papers critically was a gift from him. He treated me like his younger brother, teaching me everything he knew in medicine and cardiology. We had a small laboratory to measure patients' cardiac function; I stayed there after regular working hours and started to do research, which was uncommon for a resident. Liu was my respected and beloved teacher. In the memorial service for his death after a stroke, I told his family, friends and students in tears how much I thanked him. Without Liu, I could hardly become a cardiologist. He mentored my career at the earliest stage.

There were eight residents in the hospital. Tsu-Der Lee was a resident in the dental department. Nearly 40 years later, he became Chairman of the Board of Directors at Taipei Medical University. He was a very good dentist;

I never felt pain when he was treating my caries. We had a close friendship since we were young.

Fumi joined the hospital as one of its first pharmacists. When I was in the army, she worked as a plant manager in a local drug company named Great Asia. She was in charge of laboratory testing, manufacturing and regulatory affairs there. She gave up a relatively good salary in the drug company and took the poorly paid job at the hospital with me; we had no regrets.

Our first daughter, Ann-Lee, was born one year after we got married. After working at the hospital, Fumi supplemented our income by teaching private students to prepare for their pharmacy licensure examination. We were so busy that we had to ask my mother-in-law to take care of Ann.

In 1978, the United States announced that it would sever its formal diplomatic relationship with Taiwan and recognize the People's Republic as the legitimate representative of China. This was a big blow to the Republic of China in Taiwan, which for nearly 30 years had maintained a close tie with America.

Friendship between America and China had built gradually. In the late 1960s, war broke out between China and Russia after a border dispute. America noticed the split between these two Communist brothers and started to approach China with good will. In 1971, Taiwan's seats at the UN General Assembly and Security Council were replaced by representatives from the People's Republic. America suggested Taiwan retain a seat in the United Nations as an independent country but President Chiang refused because of his insistence on a One-China policy. He argued that there should not be two seats for China, even if the only one belonged to his enemy.

President Nixon, a long-time supporter of Chiang and Taiwan, visited China in 1972. He shook hands with Communist leaders as if they were old friends. Pictures showing his talk with Ze-Dong Mao in a library full of traditionally thread-bound Chinese books were printed on the front page of newspapers around the world.

Mao died in 1976, a year after Chiang's death in Taiwan. The 10-year-long culture revolution was over. Madam Mao and other leaders of the red guards were arrested. Madam Mao finished her own life in prison.

Nixon resigned from his presidency because of the Watergate scandal. His successor, Gerald Ford, did not win the election for the Republicans.

Democrat Jimmy Carter was elected as US president. It was his government that formally severed the official diplomatic tie with Taiwan and opened an American embassy in Beijing.

At a time when many Taiwanese felt uncertain and insecure, a grassroots movement sprang up on the island. The popularity of Western songs and dramas in Taiwan waned and local equivalents became fashionable. Hwai-Min Lin, a dancer trained in America by Martha Graham, directed his Cloud Gate Dance Theatre in a masterpiece named Legacy. Many Taiwanese, including Fumi and I, were deeply moved by the choreography, which recreated the crossing of the Taiwan Strait by our ancestors and the difficult start to their new lives on this island. The courage and perseverance of the Taiwanese were vividly portrayed on the stage.

When a representative of the American State Department came to Taiwan to discuss with Taiwanese officers the future relationship between Taiwan and the United States, many angry Taiwanese blocked his car in the street, shouted at him and threw eggs at the car.

The Taiwan Relations Act, passed by the American legislature in 1979, allowed Taiwan to purchase defensive weapons from America; Taiwan maintained an informal but special diplomatic relationship with the USA by opening a representative office in Washington DC. An American Institute in Taiwan was opened to replace the function of an American embassy. This legal document also assured Taiwan that America would defend Taiwan if Taiwan was threatened by military forces. The implication was that the source of such a threat was China.

Most countries in the world established diplomatic relationships with the People's Republic of China. Now Taiwan had a formal diplomatic relationship with only a few nations; most of them tiny developing countries in Africa, southern America or Pacific islands. The only significant exception was the Holy See, which was small but influential. The Pope was not respected as the leader of the Chinese Catholic Church in mainland China so the Vatican did not send an Apostolic Nuncio, or ambassador, there.

By following the American way, Taiwan maintained an informal but substantial diplomatic relationship with more than 100 countries in the world. International culture and economic exchange continued to flourish. Now Taiwanese passport holders have a visa-free privilege, or only require a visa upon arrival to visit most countries around the world.

CHAPTER 10

Scholarship for Studying Abroad.
Street Demonstration for Human Rights.

n the third year of my residency, I was sent to Taiwan University Hospital for three months' training in the intensive care unit. The director of that unit was Yuan-The Lee, a young, dynamic, newly promoted associate professor. In addition to managing critically ill patients, he oversaw many patients with irregular cardiac rhythm. I worked with him to analyze the electrophysiological data of these patients, sometimes till very late at night. Like Liu at Taipei Medical College Hospital, Lee taught me the most up-to-date knowledge in cardiology. He continued to support me during my career. He was the superintendent of Taiwan University Hospital at the time of his retirement.

I established the first intensive care unit at Taipei Medical College Hospital. I also carried out a survey into vibration disease among chainsaw operators in lumber-mills. Vibration might damage the nerves and result in the abnormal constriction of arteries in the hand. Numbness and pain were common symptoms; hands were pale in color and cold to touch, especially on winter days. I presented my observation at a medical conference and published a short paper on this occupational disease.

In spite of this progress, I was anxious for my future. The main reason I chose to study at the hospital of my alma mater was to become an academic physician. My long-term goal was to become a professor of medicine, as expected by myself and my family.

Even if I completed my residency at the hospital, the prospects of fulfilling my ambitions were by no means bright. Without advanced training, particularly experience in a top-tier university abroad, a young doctor could hardly climb the steep ladder of academic medicine.

My grandfather and father left me an important message: publishing research papers was the key to success in academic medicine. The only way for me to make a breakthrough was to learn medical research and publish many high-quality papers.

Taiwan University established a Graduate Institute of Clinical Medicine in 1979. Young medical doctors who completed a minimum of two years' training and published a paper could be admitted after passing an oral test. I was refused as a candidate at first, even though I was qualified according to the regulations. I argued strongly before I was allowed to take the oral test, in which my paper was heavily criticized. I was not accepted. All other candidates were graduates of Taiwan University and completed their four years' residency at their university hospital.

The Ministry of Education in Taiwan provided a government scholarship for studying abroad. It was awarded annually to a few young university graduates who passed competitive written and oral tests. The awardees were considered elites in Taiwan; their names were published in newspapers. They were obliged to work in Taiwan for two years after completing their studies abroad. If any one of them had difficulty finding a suitable job back in Taiwan, the government would help, and guarantee a satisfactory position.

Subjects for the fellowship varied from year to year, determined by the Ministry of Education and based on the needs of Taiwan. In the medical field, the scholarship was mostly given to studies in basic medicine or public health.

In 1979, I noticed that clinical pharmacology was listed as one of the subjects. Clinical pharmacology was the study of drug treatment in men; it was a relatively new discipline in medicine. Candidates were required to have a minimum of two years' training after a medical degree. I sent off the application form and became the only applicant to pass the written test. I passed the subsequent oral test smoothly. Everyone who met me congratulated me. They shared the joy and glory with me.

The Ministry would provide me with a two-year scholarship to either the USA or the UK. Fully paid tuition fees, a return ticket and monthly living allowances were all included.

There was a 'brain drain' among my generation in Taiwan. American universities offered scholarships to Taiwanese, particularly graduates from prestigious universities. Many of them stayed permanently and became American citizens.

Taiwanese medical graduates were offered jobs by American hospitals. There was a shortage of medical doctors in the USA during the Vietnam War. American hospitals actively recruited foreign medical graduates to fill their vacant positions. Many alumni of Taipei Medical College, including some of my classmates, went to the USA soon after they finished their mandatory military service. Once their clinical training was completed, they could easily become neutralized American citizens, establish a practice and enjoy their life thereafter.

Few Taiwanese medical doctors in America chose a career in medical research. Even if they did, they rarely went to a graduate school to pursue a research degree. American medical professors considered such a degree redundant. In their mind, junior doctors could learn how to do research from their seniors in the hospital. Their research experience was generally accumulated while being a fellow, which was the training after residency in a hospital.

I wrote letters to top-tier American medical institutions inquiring about training in clinical pharmacology. Most of them answered they only provided a non-degree program for fellows in the hospital. For a doctoral degree, I had to go to the department of basic pharmacology. I was disappointed.

Then I sent letters to British universities. I was warmly welcomed by several professors. Paul Turner at St. Bartholomew's Hospital answered me in only two weeks. That was very fast at the time when all correspondence was via air-mail. David Grahame-Smith at Oxford also expressed his willingness to accept me.

Turner's offer was most attractive. He would let me pursue a research degree at the University of London as a graduate student, and at the same time work as an honorary registrar to continue my clinical training at the hospital under his supervision. He also advised me to start in April 1980 so I would not have to pay the more expensive tuition fees that were being imposed on foreign students after September that year. It mattered to me so I could extend my study in London with my own savings.

Another reason for me to choose Turner's department was that clinical medicine was more advanced in London. Besides, I enjoyed the excitement of city life more than a quiet university town.

As most Taiwanese went to America for advanced studies, there was little information available in Taiwan about education and medical training in the UK.

I was fortunate to know Jau-Nan Lee, a senior gynecologist at Kaohsiung Medical College in southern Taiwan. He was studying for a doctoral degree at St. Bartholomew's Hospital. He came back to Taiwan for a winter vacation at the end of 1979. I arranged a meeting with him in Kaohsiung.

On 10 December, which the United Nations had proclaimed Human Rights Day, I took an evening train leaving Taipei. When I arrived in Kaohsiung, I was told there was a demonstration on some streets of the city so the taxi would take an alternative, but longer, route to the hotel. Street demonstrations were quite unusual at that time in Taiwan. Under martial law, the participants would be sent to prison.

Next morning, I met Lee; he kindly gave me lots of valuable advice and expressed his willingness to help if I went to London. On the train back to Taipei, I felt much more confident about my future study in England.

That street demonstration for human rights was one of the most important political events in the modern history of Taiwan. After 20 years of authoritative rule by the Nationalist Party, people in Taiwan were fed up with a fake democratic government, even though the economy in Taiwan was booming and living standards for everyone had improved. The brave demonstrators risked their lives to ask for martial law to be lifted, permission to organize new political parties, the right to vote for members of parliament, freedom of speech and, above all, freedom from the fear of political oppression. Many of the participants were arrested and prosecuted. A team of young lawyers defended them in court. A leader of the demonstration was sentenced to life imprisonment; he escaped a death penalty.

In spite of the setback, call for political reform continued; more and more people stood up to support this movement. Under great pressure, the Nationalist government changed its policy; all the requests made in that demonstration were granted a few years after I returned from London. Many participants in the demonstration and their lawyers became the new generation of political leaders. From that demonstration onwards, Taiwan started to move towards becoming a genuine democratic country.

Fumi and I left Taipei on 21 March, 1980. Fumi would accompany me to London and return to Taipei soon afterwards. This was the first time I had been abroad, but not Fumi's. During our transit in Hong Kong, I spent a few hours visiting this Chinese city ruled by the British. I took a double-decker bus from the Kai-Tak Airport to Tsim Sha Tsui at the southern tip of Kowloon; from there I saw the magnificent view of Victoria Harbor and Hong Kong Island. With great excitement, I took a Star Ferry going to the island and coming back.

We spent a week in Italy visiting Rome, Naples, Florence, and enjoying great culture, history and art. We found the marble sculptures of Michelangelo most astonishing. Before leaving Taipei, we were advised to wear simple clothes to avoid being robbed in the street. Italians wore stylish clothes; I guessed they were afraid of being robbed by us when they saw the way we were dressed.

We arrived at Heathrow Airport; from there we took the train to Oxford. We carried two heavy suitcases and managed to find how to buy tickets and change trains in a country totally different from Taiwan. We met some Taiwanese students, including Jau-Nan Lee and his family, in the house of Jason Chih-Chiang Hu, a graduate student of international relations at Balliol College. Many years later, Hu became the minister of foreign affairs in Taiwan. The total number of students from Taiwan in the UK was around 60 in the early 1980s; the total number of Taiwanese was around 300, many of them employees of Evergreen Marine, a Taiwanese cargo transportation company.

The next day, Lee drove Fumi and me to London. Before reaching the Lillian Pension Hall, a dormitory for international graduate students at the University of London, I had my first sight of St. Bartholomew's Hospital from Giltspur Street. Its five-story-high, grey stone buildings stood along the street, quiet but dignified.

PART THREE

Studying Abroad in London and Boston

CHAPTER 11

St. Bartholomew's Hospital.
Professor Turner and Gossypol.

St. Bartholomew's Hospital, known simply as Barts, is the oldest hospital in England. It has been standing on the site since Rahere founded it more than 800 years ago.

Rahere, a priest at St. Paul's Cathedral, fell seriously sick on a pilgrimage to Rome. In distress he prayed to God, promising that he would found a hospital for the poor sick in London if he was cured.

On the way back to England, he had a vision of St. Bartholomew who saved him during a terrible dream in which he was seized by a beast. The saint told Rahere to build a church and a hospital, and dedicate them to his name.

Bartholomew was one of the 12 Apostles of Jesus. In 'Last Judgment', the masterpiece painted by Michelangelo in the Sistine Chapel in the Vatican City, the artist depicted himself as St. Bartholomew after the skin of the saint had been removed alive.

Rahere got permission from King Henry I for construction in Smithfield, a few hundred meters to the north of St. Paul's Cathedral. For a long time, this land outside the city walls of London was used for hanging criminals. Visitors today can find a plate on the outer wall of Barts commemorating the execution of Sir William Wallace, the Scottish hero who fought for Scotland's independence. He was found guilty of treason, then hung, drawn and quartered at a corner of Smithfield in 1305.

Smithfield was also a place for business; merchants used to sell their products in booths. It had been famous for livestock trading before the market began to specialize in meat-cutting. Today, the UK's largest wholesale meat market is still located there.

After the Bishop of London set up a holy cross, the building of a church and a hospital started in 1123. The hospital was looked after by brothers and sisters of the church. Rahere was buried on the north side of the high altar after his death in 1143. For centuries, the sick came to the church to pray and the hospital for a cure.

In the 16th century, King Henry VIII severed relations with the Roman Catholic Church after the Pope refused to accept his divorce from his first wife. He made himself the supreme head of the Church of England. All privileges of the Catholic Church were dissolved and its possessions, including Barts, were bestowed to the King. The medical function of Barts was not interrupted, but the King re-founded the hospital in 1546. A statue of Henry VIII has been standing above the main entrance facing Smithfield since 1702.

In 1628, William Harvey, physician-in-charge of the hospital, published a book in Latin, *De Motu Cordis et Sanguinis*, or 'Motion of the heart and blood'. He reported in this book one of the greatest discoveries in medicine, the circulation of blood around the body.

Harvey graduated as a Bachelor of Arts from Cambridge; he then studied medicine in Padua, Italy. The University of Padua, founded in 1222, was the centre for learning in Europe at that time. Half a century before Harvey studied there, Andrew Vesalius established the science of modern anatomy during his tenure as professor of anatomy at this university. Harvey's advanced knowledge in anatomy played a crucial role in his discovery of circulation. Returning back to London, Harvey served at Barts until his retirement. He was physician to King James I and his ill-fated son, Charles I. Charles was beheaded after the royalists lost the civil war.

There was a long-established tradition that physicians and surgeons at the hospital taught their apprentices medicine. The regular program of medical lectures began in the 19th century. The medical college moved to new premises in Charterhouse Square near the opposite corner of Smithfield in the 20th century. Along with other medical schools attached to historic London hospitals, such as Guy's, St. George's and St. Thomas, it was incorporated into the University of London as a constituent college in the faculty of medicine. The university granted a medical degree to the graduates of all these medical colleges.

At the end of the 20th century, the University of London restructured its organization. Barts Medical College and the London Hospital Medical College in east London merged to become parts of Queen Mary College. Likewise, the medical colleges at Guy's and St. Thomas Hospitals were merged into the King's College. It was hoped that through expansion in scale and integration of resources these institutes might improve their academic competitiveness.

With more Londoners choosing to live in quiet suburban houses, there was a continuous fall in the number of residents in central London. A recommendation to close central London hospitals, including Barts, was proposed. A 'Save Barts' Campaign was mounted to fight against the threat of closure. I wrote a letter to support it; part of this letter was published in 1992 in the *Evening Standard* with a national flag of Taiwan attached to it. Barts was saved; since that episode several new buildings have been constructed to transform the hospital into a centre of excellence in cardiac and cancer medicine.

After my first meeting with Turner at his office, we walked across the square of the hospital; he opened a door of the North Wing and let me go inside. The square and its surrounding Portland-stone-covered buildings were designed by distinguished 18th-century architect James Gibbon. In front of me was the Grand Staircase, its wall dominated by two vast paintings by William Hogarth, the great English painter. They were pictures of two Bible stories: Christ's magic healing at the pool of Bethesda, and a Good Samaritan giving assistance to the injured on the roadside. Hogarth was born at Barts; he painted these pictures for the hospital free of charge between 1735 and 1737.

Upstairs was the Grand Hall, a portrait of Henry VIII hung over the fireplace, and names of benefactors who had given money to the hospital from the 16th to the early 20th century were listed on large plaques displayed on the wall. Some portraits of former physicians and surgeons were displayed on movable stands so the space could be rearranged when the hall was used for functions.

Turner brought me to the portrait of Sir Thomas Brunton, and told me how Brunton first used amyl nitrate to relieve angina chest pain in the 19th century. Amyl nitrate preceded nitroglycerine, which is still widely used for the treatment of coronary artery disease in modern hospitals today. Turner obviously considered himself as a successor to Brunton, a physician at Barts specializing in the study of drug treatment.

Turner was professor of clinical pharmacology at Barts. By the time I joined his department, he had been at the peak of his of academic career for years. He was editorial secretary to the *British Journal of Clinical Pharmacology*; graduate students from all five continents came to learn from him and contribute to his flourishing department. He was always travelling abroad as a visiting professor or chairman of international meetings.

Soon after I joined his department, Turner suggested that I study sperm. This was a great surprise to me.

Turner had the impression that the Chinese displayed talents in anything related to reproduction. China had the largest population in the world; this was evidence that Chinese knew very well how to produce children. English gentlemen gossiped about how ancient Chinese books taught men to improve their sexual performance by taking secret recipes and performing peculiar maneuvers. Most important to him was the news that Chinese scientists had developed a male contraceptive, gossypol.

Realizing that a rapidly growing population was a threat to social stability and economic growth, China took several measures to implement its population control policy. Among them was the development of a male contraceptive. Research on such a subject was practically non-existent outside China.

Gossypol was an ingredient of cotton seed oil. In some parts of China, cotton seed oil was used for cooking, after refining processes during its production. It was noticed that men became infertile if crude rather than processed oil was used in cooking. Based on such an observation, Chinese scientists purified gossypol from the oil and tested it on men. It was indeed a male contraceptive. Most of this work was carried out during the culture revolution when Chinese scientists had few interactions with the international community.

Just a few years before I arrived in London, China changed its policy and allowed senior scientists to accept invitations to present their findings at international scientific meetings. It was at a pharmacology conference Turner heard the story of gossypol and became fascinated by it.

Many years after I left Turner's department, the practice of using gossypol as a male contraceptive was proved too toxic. Weakness, with paralysis in severe cases, owing to a decreased potassium level in the blood was common; a large proportion of men who took gossypol became permanently infertile. However, Turner was indeed impressed by the enthusiasm of Chinese in studying reproduction.

Turner asked me to study whether beta-blockers, specifically propranolol, might impair male fertility. In his mind, this Chinese young man coming from Taiwan was the right person to pursue the answer to this question.

CHAPTER 12

Beta-blockers and Sir James Black. Drugs and Male Infertility.

Turner was curious to know if beta-blockers, a group of widely used cardiac drugs, might cause male infertility. This was a question puzzling many patients and their doctors.

Propranolol, the first and most popular beta-blocker, was developed by Sir James Black. A medical graduate from St. Andrews University in Scotland, Black did not go into clinical practice; instead, he joined the veterinary school at the University of Glasgow to do research. He proposed that if a chemical could block the activity of sympathetic nerves, it might slow down the heartbeat and reduce the demand for blood supply to the heart. Through this mechanism, the chemical could be developed into a drug to alleviate the symptoms of myocardial ischemia, the shortage of the blood supply to the heart muscle.

Black joined Imperial Chemical Industries, commonly known as ICI, a leading British pharmaceutical company, and during the early 1960s, assisted by the company's chemists, he developed propranolol. Clinical testing on patients with angina proved propranolol's therapeutic benefits. Additionally, it was found effective in lowering blood pressure and controlling irregular heart rhythm. Hypertension and arrhythmia were frequently associated with myocardial ischemia in patients. Propranolol, under the brand name Inderal, became a blockbuster product for ICI. It was the first of a new class of drugs called beta-adrenergic blocking agents, or beta-blockers for short. They all blocked the activity of beta-type sympathetic nerves.

Black moved to Smith, Kline and French, another big British drug company. He developed Cimetidine there during the 1970s. It was the first of another new class of drugs called H2 blockers. H2 blockers reduced the stomach's acidic secretions and became the first-choice drug for treating peptic ulcers until more potent gastric acid suppressing drugs were marketed in the 1980s.

Coronary artery disease, hypertension and peptic ulcers were highly prevalent and potentially life-threatening if not properly treated. Black's innovative mind and continuous effort relieved the suffering and saved the lives of millions all over the world. In 1988, he was awarded the Nobel Prize in Medicine for 'discoveries of important principles for drug treatment'. Gertrude Elion and George Hitchings shared the prize with him. They both worked at Wellcome Research Laboratories at Research Triangle, North Carolina, USA and developed several drugs for leukemia, gout and viral diseases.

My wife and I once visited Black at the James Black Foundation in south London. He showed us how his team of around 20 scientists was divided into two groups: one for chemical studies and the other for pharmacological studies. He also kindly drove us to the nearest Tube station in his bright red car when he knew that we had not arranged our transport back to central London.

Soon after learning that propranolol reduced heart rate, Turner tested on his patients whether this drug reduced the rapid heartbeat commonly seen in hyperthyroidism and anxiety. He published his positive results in *The Lancet* in 1965, only one year after the first clinical studies of propranolol on angina and hypertension were reported.

Since Black developed propranolol in the 1960s, beta-blockers had become the most important drugs in treating cardiovascular diseases. Big drug companies developed their own brands of beta-blockers, and sales of beta-blockers were very profitable. The careers of many medical scientists, including Turner, developed based on their research of beta-blockers.

No wonder Turner and many others with a stake in beta-blockers were concerned when speculation grew that, in sporadic cases, beta-blockers may cause male infertility. The idea that beta-blockers might cause impotence was well established, because men felt tired after the activity of their heart was suppressed by a beta-blocker. Many patients asked their physicians to swap to other types of drugs even if their chest pain, high blood pressure or irregular heartbeat were well controlled by a beta-blocker.

It was bad news if life-saving beta-blockers made men infertile in addition to causing impotence.

There are many causes of male infertility, some hereditary, some environmental, some disease-related and some drug-induced. Examples of causative agents include heavy metals, irradiation, anti-cancer agents and hormones, etc.

There was a theoretical basis to the belief that beta-blockers could induce infertility. It was generally accepted that beta-blockers reduced cellular cyclic AMP through a cascade of enzymatic activities. Cyclic AMP was discovered by an American professor, Earl Sutherland, who won a Nobel Prize in medicine in 1971 for the discovery. Cyclic AMP is a chemical that regulates many cellular functions, including the supply of energy to cells.

Sperm have to swim from the cervix where semen was ejaculated to an ovarian end of the uterine tube to fertilize an egg. This movement requires energy. If beta-blockers reduced intracellular cyclic AMP, this could in turn reduce the energy supply to sperm; sperm might then become less motile and fail to fertilize an egg. The widely known fact that caffeine, a chemical that increases cyclic AMP, stimulated sperm motility in the test tube further supported the hypothesis that beta-blockers might render sperm less motile by decreasing cyclic AMP.

William Hendry, consultant urologist at Barts, told Turner that some of his patients complained to him that they tried unsuccessfully to conceive a child after taking a beta-blocker. To encourage my interest in this topic, Turner asked Hendry to let me watch how this busy surgeon treated his private patients in a Harley Street clinic. British medical doctors serving in National Health Service hospitals were allowed a few hours to engage in private practice, and Harley Street in central London was where such practices flourished. Many rich and/or powerful patients from Commonwealth countries and former British colonies came here to seek the best medical treatment. During the 1990s, Hendry became the president of British Association of Urological Surgeons.

When Turner first suggested that I study sperm, I was surprised and found it difficult to accept. My reluctance to choose sperm as my research subject was straightforward: how could I have come all the way from Taiwan to London, expecting to study cardiovascular drugs, and end up studying sperm? Surely it was a topic more suitable for a urologist or an obstetrician/gynecologist. Turner reminded me the research was into beta-blockers, the most widely used group of cardiovascular drugs. Finally I accepted his assignment; I really did not have other options.

Turner and I designed several models to explore the potential adverse effects of beta-blockers on sperm. We considered conducting a clinical study to compare the sperm quality of patients taking a beta-blocker with that of those who did not take the drug. A large scale clinical trial would need a lot of resources: getting hospital approval, recruiting patients, giving them drugs, following them up and examining their specimens. We did not have the time or the funding to complete such a trial. But if we conducted a small-scale trial, we would be criticized that we were unable to reach a firm conclusion because our patient numbers were limited.

We then thought we should try an animal study. A technician was assigned to help me set up equipment for experiments in the pharmacology department. Only small animals, such as rabbits and rats, could be accommodated in the laboratory. It proved impossible for me to take the tiny testis intact from these poor creatures. Besides, the rationale for such experiments was questionable.

The next attempt involved getting a fresh human specimen. I waited outside the operation room for a diseased testis, just removed by Hendry. It was, however, very rare that a man would like to be castrated, even if only one of his two testes was involved. So this approach was prematurely terminated.

Several months passed. I fell into despair. The excitement of coming to London gradually faded away. Alone in London, I was away from my wife and daughter whom I missed very much. There were few Mandarin-speaking Chinese to talk to; most Chinese in London came from Hong Kong and spoke in Cantonese dialect rather than the official Mandarin Chinese commonly used in Taiwan and China. The food in London did not appeal to me. There was a famous comment that the only way to enjoy British food was to choose breakfast for all meals. Chinese food served in London's 'Chinatown' was also foreign to me. It was either too sweet, characteristic of Hong Kong Cantonese food; or plain in taste, despite their variations of color and ingredients.

My last resort was to measure the effect of beta-blockers on sperm after mixing semen with the drug in a test tube. Hendry introduced me to Javoslava Parslow who was in charge of the semen laboratory at Barts. 'Yaya' was the nickname of this Czech lady. She married an Englishman and left Prague after the anti-Communist uprising in 1968. The semen laboratory not only served urology patients by examining their semen quality, but also provided gynecology patients with semen obtained from donors for artificial insemination. In vitro fertilization had yet to become a standard medical procedure, even though the first test tube baby, Louise Brown, was born in 1978, mainly thanks to the pioneering research of Robert Edward in Cambridge. Edward was awarded a Nobel Prize in 2010, but he was too old to receive the prize from the Swedish king in person.

Turner borrowed a microscope for me to use in our department. I regularly got semen samples from the semen laboratory. The question I faced at this stage was how to measure the effects of drugs on sperm motility.

The term 'sperm' was derived from a Greek word meaning seed. In Chinese, it was called 'exquisite worm'. Sperm was mysterious to scientists and laymen alike; it was one of the first cells curiously examined by Antonie van Leeuwenhoek, the Dutchman who invented a microscope in the 17th century. When I started to study sperm motility, the laboratory computer was rudimentary and computer image analysis was yet to be developed. Measurement of sperm motility was not much changed since Leeuwenhoek's time; direct visual observation was still the standard method of judging if sperm motility in semen was good. This was qualitative at best, definitely not quantitative. One could see the difference between sperm swimming vigorously and those swimming in a tiresome fashion; but it was hard to tell those in between. Besides, a large number of sperm in semen were examined at the same time. They were swimming at different speeds in different directions. The subjective and arbitrary natures of visual assessment were well recognized, but it was still widely used in the clinic mainly because it was easy to do. When describing my work to my colleagues, I likened the measurement of sperm motility under the microscope to sitting on top of Eros' statue in the centre of Piccadilly Circus in London and counting how many people around the circus were walking fast, slowly, or not at all. You could hardly be accurate.

A colleague from Hungary, Irene Kovac, introduced me to the laboratory of Professor Gustav Born at King's College on London's Strand. Her husband worked with Born. Born invented a platelet aggregometer to measure drug-induced change in human platelets. This instrument made the development of platelet inhibitors possible; and eventually led to the universal use of aspirin in the prevention of strokes and heart attacks. I was amazed to see how simple the principles and the instruments of this classic laboratory test were.

Convinced that simple was beautiful, I returned to Barts. On the entrance to the hospital library, I noticed an inscription: 'Whatsoever your hand finds to do, do it with all your might'. There must be many former Barts students inspired by this quotation; some of them became Nobel laureates. I should be persistent, regardless of how sperm research might impact my career.

CHAPTER 13

Human Sperm Motility.
Heart Drugs and Coke as Contraceptives.

Around half a year after I came to London, I succeeded in developing a trans-membrane migration method to measure sperm motility objectively and quantitatively.

I invented a simple apparatus. It was made from two parts: a semen container on the top and a saline container at the bottom. Between them was a special Nuclepore membrane with many evenly distributed, laser-punctured 5-micrometer pores in it.

The whole apparatus was put into a water bath for two hours. During this time, motile sperm in the semen would swim across the tiny pores in the membrane into the saline. Sperm heads were 3 micrometers in diameter, so only one sperm could pass through a 5-micrometer pore at one time. If sperm in semen were killed before the experiment, none of them would appear in the saline, indicating that only motile sperm crossed the membrane. In such condition, the tiny pores could all be blocked by dead sperm which lay flat on the membrane.

At the end of two hours, the sperm numbers in the saline were counted. The number of sperm in the semen was counted before the experiment, so the percentage of sperm that moved across the membrane from semen to saline could be calculated. This trans-membrane migration ratio expressed as a percentage was an indicator for sperm motility.

An average semen sample was around 3ml in volume. Since each measurement required 0.1ml of semen, one sample could be divided into more than 20 aliquots. Different drugs at different concentrations could be compared without interference due to variation in different semen samples.

A series of experiments was carried out to prove this method not only measured sperm motility accurately, but also precisely. The latter was an expression of its reproducibility, the degree to which repeated measurements gave the same results. In this respect, the trans-membrane migration method was far superior to the traditional, subjective visual assessment. The stimulatory effect of caffeine on sperm motility was demonstrated with this new method, confirming the finding of previous investigations. Turner and I published our method in a letter to the *British Journal of Clinical Pharmacology*. The third author, Mark Chaput de Saintonge, was a consultant at Barts; he taught me statistical analysis of laboratory data.

I mixed dissolved propranolol at different concentrations with semen and found a concentration-dependent inhibitory effect of this drug on sperm motility. At a concentration of millimolar range, propranolol stopped all sperm movement. In fact, I was able to observe under the microscope sperm lying motionless once they were mixed with propranolol. I tested other types of beta-blockers; some inhibited sperm motility, but some did not, and none of them were as potent as propranolol.

Turner was relieved to know that not all beta-blockers inhibited sperm motility. Being an expert in beta-blockers, he soon pointed out to me after reading my data that local anesthetic effect of a drug, not the sympathetic nerve blocking activity, made sperm immotile in my experiments.

Local anesthetic activity, also known as membrane stabilizing activity, was an effect present in many types of drugs. At high concentrations (unlikely to be attainable in the human body), some beta-blockers might have this effect. This effect was, however, totally independent of the therapeutic benefits of beta-blockers.

Since cellular membranes were made mainly of lipids, the ability of a drug to change the structure of a cell membrane and 'anesthetize' or 'stabilize' it was dependent on its solubility in the lipid. Among beta-blockers, propranolol was the most lipid-soluble one; no wonder it was most potent in inhibiting sperm motility. My data showed that the inhibitory effect of beta-blockers on sperm motility correlated well with their lipid solubility. Lipid-insoluble beta-blockers could hardly inhibit sperm motility.

At millimolar range, the concentration required for any beta-blocker to inhibit sperm motility was extremely high. Concentrations of beta-blockers in blood were normally in micromolar ranges. A micromolar was one-thousandth of a millimolar. Even 10 micromolar was only one-hundredth of a millimolar. I concluded that beta-blockers were unlikely to suppress male fertility by inhibiting sperm motility because they could hardly achieve the toxic concentration. Doctors and patients did not need to worry about it.

A full-length paper was accepted by the *British Journal of Clinical Pharmacology*. I tested several other drugs with local anesthetic activities, such as tranquilizers and antiarrhythmic agents, and proved that they all inhibited sperm motility. Some of them were no less potent than propranolol. One by one, my papers were published in leading medical journals. It was said that a science came of age when it became quantitative. A quantitative method was the key to scientific research and I invented one. From then on, I was able to enjoy London more.

Fumi came from Taipei to join me. We rented a room in Yao-Sheng Chen's house in Golders Green. Chen came from a wealthy family in the Yangtze River Delta, the richest area in China. He served in the Chinese Embassy in London before Communists took over China. He and his wife were active among overseas Chinese in London. He invested in a restaurant serving genuine banquet dishes while she opened a Sunday school in the church for kids to learn Chinese. They had never rented a room to a Taiwanese before; they were happy to have a medical doctor staying and taking care of their health. Their daughters were married and their only son, studying at Cambridge, died in a rock-climbing accident.

Smoking his pipe, Chen told me many stories of London and taught me how to enjoy British culture. During weekends, Fumi and I walked on Hampstead Heath and read the *Sunday Times Magazine* on a wooden bench in the park. Fumi worked as a locum pharmacist at St. Leonard's Hospital where James Parkinson first described a degenerative disease of the nervous system characterized with muscle rigidity, hand tremors and difficulty walking in 1817. Originally called shaking palsy, this disease was later named after him.

With Fumi's income to supplement my scholarship, we could afford to enjoy shops, museums and theaters in London. We travelled to provincial cities and continental Europe. We shared the British celebration of the wedding of Charles and Diana, and trying to find an alternative route to our workplaces when London public transport took industrial action against the policies of Margret Thatcher.

The libraries in the hospital and medical school at Barts were inadequate for me to get all the references for my research. Recommended by Turner, I joined the Royal Society of Medicine as a fellow. I spent many days and nights studying there. Its vast library was a paradise for scholars. Books on all branches of medicine and journals dating back to the19th century were stocked and waiting silently for the readers.

Turner told me that I was ready to write a thesis for a PhD degree from the University of London. When I first registered at the university, I was admitted as a master's student. At the end of my first year, Turner was satisfied with my progress and recognized that my qualification was equivalent to a student holding a master's degree. He retrospectively switched my status to a PhD student. Under the regulations of the university at that time, the minimum requirement to obtain a PhD degree was to finish two years' full-time research at an institute of the university, write a thesis and pass the oral test.

I tried hard to complete the whole process as fast as possible. I did not want to spend my savings to extend my study in London beyond the two-year limit of the government scholarship from Taiwan.

The viva, or oral test, lasted for two hours. I had been worried that I might not be able to understand some of the questions because my colloquial English was not fluent enough. Fortunately, the examiners were kind, albeit critical.

To my knowledge, I was the second Taiwanese medical graduate ever to receive a doctoral degree from the UK. The first one, Ming T. Tsuang, 17 years my senior, studied psychiatry in London and spent his entire academic career in American universities.

Turner once teased me that I could not see the difference between 'he' and 'she' even after I received my PhD. He was right; I always mixed up 'he' with 'she' during my talk in English. In spoken Chinese, there was no difference between male and female gender. However, Turner did praise my English writing; he said that my English grammar was much better than most British. My English teacher in the junior high school should be credited for it.

I was in great debt to some of my colleagues at Barts. Shortage of semen samples of acceptable quality was always a problem for me. Semen banks need good-quality semen from donors for artificial insemination; while poor-quality semen from patients was not suitable for my experiments. Some colleagues volunteered to give me their semen. I advised them to collect samples in a small, wide-mouthed plastic jar. They either left the jar on my bench anonymously or handed it to me in person.

On winter days, I found that most sperm in the jars were frozen to death. Most likely it happened during my colleagues' trip from their houses to the hospital. I gave them a test tube and asked them to wait for a few minutes until the initially jelly-like semen in the jar had liquefied, then pour it into the test tube. 'Keep the test tube warm in an inner pocket of your jacket on your way to the hospital,' I said. They were happy to learn how to keep sperm alive and followed my tips.

The whole research project of mine was not supported by any grant; Turner paid all the expenses for equipment and chemicals from the departmental budget. Without the goodwill of many friends, my research could not have progressed smoothly.

Among them, Atholl Johnston, who later became professor of clinical pharmacology at Barts, was always helpful in my experimental work. In 2008, he reported that the blood sample of Princess Diana's driver in her fatal car accident probably belonged to someone else. The media widely quoted his announcement and the public questioned again whether Diana had been murdered.

A special friend, Salim Hassan, came from Iraq. A medical graduate from Baghdad, he was at Barts to pursue an advanced research degree. Before meeting him, I knew little about the Muslim and Arabian world. We often chatted and dined together in the hospital canteen. Like me, he left his wife at home during his first few months in London. He was one of my volunteer donors. At first, his semen had the highest number of sperm I had ever seen. However, after his wife joined him in London, I noticed a continuous fall in his sperm concentration, although it was still within normal limits. I often joked with him about this dramatic change, but he continued to donate samples to me. He was very kind and humorous. I lost contact with him a few years later; it was my sincere hope that he survived all the difficulties many Iraqi people suffered.

In addition to a PhD degree, I got an AMAPI (Association of Medical Advisers in Pharmaceutical Industry) Prize from the Clinical Section of the British Pharmacological Society in 1982. Each year, only one clinical pharmacologist under 35 who published the best paper was awarded the prize, the name of which was later changed to BrAPP (British Association for Pharmaceutical Physicians) Prize.

After I returned to Taiwan, Turner and his colleagues at Barts continued research into propranolol and fertility. They measured propranolol concentrations simultaneously in blood and semen after volunteers took the drug. It was found that drug concentrations were comparable in these two fluids. This was not an easy job for the volunteers: they had to present semen samples at hours one, two, four and eight of the experiment. This study reassured that propranolol, the most potent beta-blocker in inhibiting sperm motility, was unlikely to reach sperm-immobilizing levels either in blood or semen at a therapeutic dose.

Turner and his colleagues also found that propranolol could accumulate in cervicovaginal mucus after oral administration because of the acidic medium of the vagina. Its concentration, however, was still too low to immobilize sperm.

A clinical trial was carried out in Chile to see if propranolol could be used as a vaginal contraceptive. It was published in 1983 in the *British Medical Journal*. The media was excited to print 'heart drug is an effective contraceptive' as a headline. News reporters in Taiwan called me and asked for my comments; they knew my research in London was closely related to this topic.

Nearly 200 fertile women were asked to insert an 80mg propranolol tablet into their vagina each evening during their menstruation-free days for up to 11 months. Propranolol was indeed found to be an effective vaginal contraceptive. The high concentration required to immobilize sperm could be reached when the propranolol tablet was dissolved in the vagina. Side-effects reported by these women were mostly itching or discomfort in the vagina, which could be due to the local anesthetic effect of propranolol on vagina mucosa.

Turner was curious to see how propranolol was absorbed after being dissolved in the vagina. Investigators at Barts found this drug was extremely well absorbed from the vagina into the blood. Blood concentration was much higher after vaginal administration than when propranolol was taken orally. Drugs absorbed from the vagina entered systemic circulation directly, while drugs absorbed from the digestive tract had to pass through the liver first. Many drugs including propranolol were metabolized and became inactive in the liver.

The lack of so called 'first pass metabolism' for vaginal-administered propranolol was the reason for its higher concentration in blood levels. This observation raised a safety concern that propranolol could not be used in women as a vaginal contraceptive if they had contra-indications for beta-blockers, such as asthma or a slow heart rate. No drug companies were ready to market propranolol as a contraceptive but research in the field continued. In 2012, a group of scientists in Iran reported that they had developed a vaginal adhesive propranolol gel with prolonged contraceptive efficacy.

After returning to Taipei, I continued research into sperm motility for several years. I read a short paper from a Harvard team in the *New England Journal of Medicine*. They claimed that Coke had a spermicidal effect. They did this research because Coke was used by some couples in developing countries as a vaginal douche after sex to prevent pregnancy. They used Coke in a glass bottle with a neck, not the canned variety. After vigorous shaking, the thumb was released from the top of the bottle and a jet of Coke flushed into the vagina.

I was curious about this report. Under my supervision, my colleagues tested several types of Cola including classical Coke, caffeine-free Coke and Pepsi-Cola using the trans-membrane migration method. Their potencies in inhibiting sperm motility were all very weak. We published a paper to reject the contraceptive value of Coke and warn against such a practice because of its risk of infection.

Twenty years later in 2008, the Ig Nobel Prize in chemistry was awarded to me, my co-authors and the team in Harvard on our research into Coke. This prize was given annually to research that first made people laugh and then made them think. My younger daughter Wan, working in New York, received the award for me at the Sanders Theater of Harvard University. She told the audience that she was born because her parents failed in contraception. This event attracted worldwide media coverage. Most awardees, including me, found it amusing, even though there was a sense of satire to it. In 1995, the Ig Nobel Prize award for peace was given to the Taiwanese legislature; citing that punching and kicking inside parliament was much better than waging war against other nations.

When I was sure that I could earn a PhD degree from London, I wrote a letter to Benjamin Bi-Ning Chiang, then chief of cardiology at Taipei Veterans General Hospital and professor of medicine at National Yang-Ming Medical College in Taipei. I asked him if I could work in his department upon my return to Taiwan. He immediately answered me and welcomed me sincerely. He did not ask me for more information, such as referees, recommendation letters, or supporting documents. No one introduced me to him in private. That was unusual for any Taiwanese institute to hire new staff. I was very happy to get a good job in Taiwan. After staying in London for 25 months, I boarded a flight at Heathrow Airport to travel back home.

CHAPTER 14

Veterans General Hospital and Yang-Ming. Improving Research Quality.

I t was traditional for a medical centre in Taiwan to hire an attending physician only if he received his resident training at the hospital. This policy of maintaining a pure pedigree was claimed to guarantee the quality of the hospital; only those who passed all the tests during their resident years could be trusted. In reality, this was the best way to guarantee the authority of the seniors. Chinese students were taught to follow an old saying: one day as a teacher, a lifetime as a father. If those who joined later were former students, they would never offend the seniors.

It was therefore extraordinary for me to become an attending physician at Taipei Veterans General Hospital, or VGH in short. I had never worked there before. The phrase 'landing by helicopter, not climbing the hill', was used to describe such a situation.

VGH was originally built by the government to take care of veterans who mostly followed Kai-Shek Chiang from mainland China to Taiwan. Open to general public and located in the northern suburb of Taipei, it boasted generous support from the government as well as the most up-to-date medical facilities.

The only hospital comparable to VGH in scale was the National Taiwan University Hospital, originally built by the Japanese. It was absolutely closed to graduates from any other medical school; its residents were picked from graduates of its own medical school, and attending doctors were residents who had completed clinical training in its hospital.

A National Yang-Ming Medical College was built in the neighborhood of VGH. VGH was the teaching hospital for Yang-Ming and attending physicians at VGH were appointed into clinical faculties at Yang-Ming. As an MD-PhD, I was qualified to be an associate professor. MDs without a PhD had to start as lecturers.

The year I joined Yang-Ming, its first class of medical students graduated. They all received government scholarships so had to serve in assigned public hospitals for seven years after graduation. A few years later, students paying their own fees (without this service obligation) were also enrolled.

Professor Bi-Ning Chiang, or Benjamin as his foreign friends called him, was a medical graduate of Defense Medical College. After training in cardiology at the National Heart Hospital in London, he went to the University of Michigan at Ann Arbor, USA and published there a landmark paper on the relationship between ventricular premature beats and mortality, based on data from the Tecumseh population study. Before going to London, I listened with admiration to his lectures at several medical conferences. His presentations were always concise and clear.

In addition to clinical service and teaching responsibilities, I was given a laboratory space and an assistant to start my research. I also had my first research fellow, Shing-Jong Lin. Lin had just finished his resident training in internal medicine and started his specialty training in cardiology. Benjamin assigned him to my laboratory to get research training. Assisted by colleagues in the biochemistry department, we prepared red blood cell membranes to see if there was any difference between normal subjects and hypertensive patients in the enzymatic activity of transporting electrolytes. We published a paper on Clinical and Experimental Hypertension in the USA with his name listed as the first author. It was extremely rare for a junior Taiwanese medical doctor to publish a scientific paper in an international journal at that time.

Lin was a hard-working man, only a few years younger than me. He later went to New York to get a PhD from Columbia University. Now he is Chief of the Research Department at VGH, Dean of research at Yang-Ming and President of the Taiwan Society of Cardiology. Among those who had worked with me in my laboratory, he was the most outstanding in terms of academic achievement.

Lin's supervisor in the United States was Shu Chien, one of the most eminent Taiwanese-American medical scientists. Chien was born in mainland China; he completed medical school in Taiwan before going to the United States to develop a brilliant academic career including the presidency of the American Physiological Society. In 2011, aged 80, he received a US National Medal of Science from President Obama. He is still very active at the University of California, San Diego.

Chien's father was a former president of Taiwan University. One of his two brothers was minister of foreign affairs while the other one was minister of finance in Taiwan. Although born into such a family, Chien nevertheless had a very warm and kind personality. Once I witnessed how considerate he was.

On the first day Lin reported to Chien's department at Columbia University, I was in New York so I accompanied Lin to visit Chien and took a look at Lin's dorm room. We were surprised to find a refrigerator full of food prepared by Chien and his wife. Who could imagine a professor treating his graduate student just arriving from abroad like this?

I still researched sperm at VGH even though I was working clinically in a cardiac department. This was only possible thanks to Benjamin's understanding. He respected academic freedom and let me do whatever project I considered appropriate. I did not disappoint him.

Calcium-blockers were drugs that reduced the flow of calcium into the cell. Like beta-blockers, they were widely used in the treatment of cardiovascular diseases, such as angina chest pain, high blood pressure and irregular heart rhythm. My experiments with calcium-blockers and other calcium-regulating agents resulted in a series of papers reporting the relation between calcium and sperm motility.

In 1984, two years after I returned to Taiwan, I summarized my findings and those of others and published a review in *The Lancet* titled 'Calcium ion is the key regulator of human sperm function'. Contrary to the concept popular during the 1970s that cyclic AMP played the most important role in sperm functions including motility, in this paper I emphasized the role of calcium. With progress in molecular and cellular techniques, more and more research on the role of calcium in sperm function has been published since I wrote my *Lancet* paper. I was very glad to read about this progress.

In 1983, I made my first trip to the USA to attend the Second World Conference of Clinical Pharmacology and Therapeutics in Washington DC. There I happily met with Turner and other colleagues coming from London. I enjoyed the Smithsonian museums, straight and wide boulevards, casual and relaxed air, and American food, charcoal-grilled steak in particular.

Coming back to Taipei from the States, I wrote a report for the hospital. That was required if the trip was supported by a grant from the hospital. I made some suggestions to improve the quality of research in the hospital. Superintendent Ji-Xun Tsou carefully read my report, wrote comments and distributed it to all department heads in the hospital.

First, I suggested that research papers should be submitted to international journals for external peer review. Most medical colleges in Taiwan published their own journals to which faculty members submitted their papers. Editors and reviewers were all insiders. Senior professors used the journals to maintain their authority in the campus. Because promotion to a higher academic rank was judged by the number and quality of papers published, a senior professor sitting on the editorial board could clone his own clan by rejecting papers submitted from staff he disliked. Circulation of such journals was extremely limited. It was joked that only reviewers, the editor and the writer read the paper.

Second, research grants should be distributed based on the merit of research proposals; the merit should be evaluated by a committee of members with sound research experience, not by department heads who knew little about research. Departments and individuals with better research performance should get more grants. Research grants should not be a budget evenly rationed to all departments.

Third, I wished to encourage young physicians to do research and give financial support to the selected few with a research potential to pursue a PhD. I also suggested starting a MD-PhD program at Yang-Ming Medical College.

This report was widely publicized by the media and led to turmoil among senior staff at VGH. Some of them felt insulted or threatened. They criticized me as a rude and proud newcomer, reconfirming their idea that the hospital should never hire someone who had not been tamed before in the hospital.

It did not take long to see that what I suggested was common sense. When I wrote that report, VGH staff published only five papers a year in international medical journals, now the number is over 1,000.

I was awarded best researcher at VGH and appointed as deputy director when a clinical research centre was founded in the hospital. Academia

Sinica, the highest scholarly organization in Taiwan, supported Taiwan University Medical College, Defense Medical College and Yang-Ming Medical College to establish a clinical research centre at their teaching hospitals. It was a turning point indicating that Taiwanese government started to promote clinical research actively. Benjamin was the director of the centre; he authorized me to sign for him on most routine documents.

Benjamin Chiang was my boss, guardian and mentor. Sometimes, we sat down to talk about the classic Chinese poems and literature we both enjoyed. Once I made a harsh comment on a piece of a document prepared by a colleague. He advised me to discuss with the colleague to explain why I could not accept the proposal before writing my decision on the paper. Regarded by many as the most powerful man in medicine because of his position as physician-in-charge to the president in Taiwan, he was a gentleman skilful in management and kind in consideration for others.

Family life during my four years as an associated professor was happy and memorable. Our younger daughter, Wan-Ching, was born in 1984. I learned to drive and bought our first car, a used Honda Civic. The hospital built new apartments for medical doctors; we moved in as some of the first occupants. Fumi worked as a manager for consumer products at Proctor and Gamble, which had just begun trading in Taiwan. She gave Pampers, the baby diaper, a Chinese name, 'Help Baby Comfort'. It sounds like Pampers when pronounced in Chinese.

However, I gradually faced a career bottleneck. I knew that sperm could not be my research subject any more. The success of *in vitro* fertilization invited many scientists and institutions to study sperm; my resources in the cardiac department were limited for me to compete with them in sperm research. Besides, the introduction of computerized image analysis for studying sperm motility made my trans-membrane migration method outdated. Unless I engaged all my efforts on sperm, I would soon lose my advantage as a leading sperm researcher. This option, however, was not feasible for me.

It was time for me to search for another research subject. In 1986, I submitted my application for promotion to full professor. Before it was officially approved, I wanted to spend some time abroad learning new research methodologies so I could continue to do research and publish papers in the future.

The National Science Council in Taiwan awarded me a grant to spend six months in a research institute abroad. I sent a letter to Edgar Haber at the cardiac unit of Massachusetts General Hospital, the major teaching hospital of Harvard University. He kindly accepted me.

CHAPTER 15

Massachusetts General Hospital. Purifying Adrenergic Receptors.

On a freezing winter day in early 1987, my whole family arrived at Boston. My daughters were excited, but I tried to keep them indoors, avoiding any possibility we might need to visit a hospital and pay the sky-high American medical costs. We got health insurance after I became a member of the Massachusetts General Hospital.

This hospital, commonly called MGH, was opened in 1811. It was the original teaching hospital for the medical school of Harvard University. After the medical school moved to a new campus in the early 20th century, several new teaching hospitals were built, mostly near the medical school in the Longwood medical area. However, MGH remained Harvard's largest teaching hospital.

Among MGH's legacies, perhaps the most famous is the first operation carried out under general anesthesia in 1846. The invention of the painless operation was the first medical breakthrough made in the United States. From then on, Americans were no longer followers; they started to lead medical progress. Prior to that, American physicians and surgeons could only get advanced training in Europe. Ether Dome, where this historic event happened, is the landmark and symbol of the hospital.

My title at Harvard was 'research fellow'. I might have been overqualified for this appointment, but I did not mind; I came here to learn something brand new to me: molecular cardiology.

The cardiac unit at MGH was founded by Paul White after he returned from postgraduate study at University College Hospital, London in 1914.

He became the most famous and respected American cardiologist of his age. In addition to his service at MGH and Harvard, he made a great contribution to the establishment of the American Heart Association and the National Heart Institute in the USA.

Edgar Haber was the chief of cardiology when I was at MGH. My first impression was that he looked like President Lincoln, only shorter. He accepted an invitation to be the chief of cardiology when he was doing research at the National Heart Institute in Bethesda, Maryland. He took another year of medical residency at MGH and a year of cardiology training at St. George's Hospital in London before he took the position aged 32.

My supervisor at the cardiac unit's cellular and molecular research laboratory was Robert Graham, a young physician-scientist from Australia. Before coming to Boston, he published a paper describing the first dose effect of prazosin, an anti-hypertensive drug. Shortly after a patient took the first dose of this drug, there could be a sudden and sharp fall in blood pressure, particularly when he changed his body position from lying to standing. This was most dangerous for the elderly if it happened at night. They may faint or fall, resulting in body injury. In most cases, this side effect did not recur after the initial period of therapy.

I was involved in a project about the isolation and purification of alpha receptor, the site in a cell where an alpha-blocking drug exerts its effects. My PhD thesis in London was focused on beta-blockers. In Boston, the subject changed to alpha-blockers. Graham knew alpha receptors much better than others because his early work was on prazosin, the prototype alpha-blocker. We sacrificed rats and took out their livers which were rich in alpha-receptors. Isolation and purification were tedious work, time-consuming for each experimental step. I did learn many laboratory techniques, but they were mostly available at biochemical laboratories in Taiwan. I was disappointed that our project had nothing to do with DNA, RNA or genes; knowledge and methodology in these areas were the mainstream in molecular research and more likely to complement my future career in Taiwan.

What bothered me more was the question in my mind: 'What is the clinical relevance of this project?' Clinical meant patient-related. As a clinical scientist, I was taught to ask clinical questions, even if the question needed laboratory work to answer it. Purification of alpha-receptors might have clinical relevance, but it was definitely remote. No one at MGH could tell me the clinical question this project was going to answer. After I left Boston, Graham's team at MGH did not succeed in purifying the alpha-receptor. This work was completed by Robert Lefkowitz at Duke University. Lefkowitz was awarded a Nobel Prize in chemistry, not in medicine, in 2012 for his serial research into receptors.

To my great surprise, and probably many others as well, in 1988 Haber left MGH to join Squibb, a big pharmaceutical company later merged with others to become Bristol Myers Squibb. He became president of its research institute. He did not stay there long; three years later he returned to Harvard as director of a new Centre for the Prevention of Cardiovascular Diseases at the School of Public Health. I met him at a dinner banquet when he visited Taipei. He died of cancer in his sixties before he retired.

Graham moved from MGH to Cleveland. In 1994 he went back to Australia as the inaugural executive director of the Victor Chang Cardiac Research Institute in Sydney. Chang was born in Shanghai, China. A leading cardiac surgeon in Australia, Chang died tragically after being shot by two robbers from Malaysia.

Although I was frustrated in my progress in the laboratory, I quite enjoyed life in Boston. Much smaller than London, Boston's charm was its combination of England and America. My family and I frequently drove to the nearby towns at weekends. Ann studied at Quincy Elementary School in Chinatown and Wan at Boston Children's School near our apartment in Charles River Park. Unlike in London, Fumi did not work in Boston; she spent all her time taking care of the family.

Tsong-Teoh Yang, my classmate at junior high school, studied pharmacy in Taiwan before migrating to the USA. After obtaining a PhD in pharmaceutical sciences, he worked for Schering-Plough, an American drug company that later merged with Merck. At Schering-Plough he specialized in drug formulation and developed an inhaler for powdered medication to treat asthma. My family spent several weekends in his house in New Jersey. He and his family, including two boys, accompanied us for sightseeing in New York. Twenty years later, his elder son became a successful neurosurgeon. After retirement, Yang acted as a consultant in Taiwan and assisted in drug development for Taiwanese companies.

Yang was a typical example of how Taiwanese of our generation studied, worked and lived in the United States. Many of them studied electrical engineering, or double E as it was often called, and worked in the computer industry. They contributed greatly to the rapid growth of science and technology in America. After a successful career in the USA, some of them flew frequently between both sides of the Pacific and participated in business development and economic growth in Taiwan and China.

A few Taiwanese were very successful in the United States. For example, Yuan-Tseh Li won the 1986 Nobel Prize in chemistry. He returned to Taiwan and became the president of Academia Sinica, the highest scholarly organization in Taiwan, roughly equivalent to the Royal Society in the UK.

Ang Lee, a film director who twice won the best director Oscar, was indeed the Taiwanese-American I respected most. I was moved each time I watched his masterpieces such as *Crouching Tiger Hidden Dragon*, *Brokeback Mountain*, *Lust, Caution* and *Life of Pi*. He was skilful in probing the depths of human nature. Some of his films contained strong Chinese elements, while others were rich in flavors foreign to most Taiwanese. In every one of them, he showed an artistic sophistication and a sense of empathy toward the others. He achieved the highest standard of culture; he was a pride to every Taiwanese.

In the 21st century, few Taiwanese go to the USA to pursue a PhD. Nowadays, most young Taiwanese complete both their undergraduate and postgraduate degrees in Taiwan. Many American universities are now full of students from China.

Bookshops in Boston were my favorite place to spend my free time. I found their books on business and management most interesting. My work back in Taiwan was very much influenced by these books. It was in Boston I learned entrepreneurship, which was worshiped at the business-oriented Harvard.

Overall, I liked England much better than New England. Someone told me that a Chinese person could easily adapt to life in the USA or the UK, but if he went to one of them first, he might have more difficulty in the second one, compared with going directly to the second one. This was most likely because his culture shock at going abroad had been pre-conditioned by the first trip.

The travelling grant I received from Taiwan lasted six months, but my contract with Harvard/MGH was one-year-long. In Taiwan, I got approval to extend my stay in Boston. One summer day, I received a letter from Yang-Ming Medical College informing me that my promotion to the rank of full professor had been approved by the Ministry of Education in Taiwan. I could not wait to go back to Taipei. The expectation of my grandfather and father to have a medical professor in our family had been fulfilled. I was just over 38 years old, exceptionally young for a professor in Taiwan. After nine months in Boston, my whole family returned to Taipei.

Before leaving the States, we took a trip to several cities in America. In Baltimore, Maryland, I visited Johns Hopkins Hospital, the Mecca of medicine in my mind since I was a young medical student. The medical institution and the university were great, but the rundown inner city on our way to the hospital astonished me.

Sometimes I wondered what would have happened to me if I had stayed in the United States to develop my career. My father was considering helping me to find a training position in USA before he passed away. I chose a British university instead of an American one when I was granted a government fellowship allowing me to study in either country. I came to Harvard and terminated my contract with it prematurely.

To many in the world, the American dream was their ultimate destiny. My father was asked if he would like to continue his study at Johns Hopkins after finishing his master's degree, like many Taiwanese did at that time. He returned to Taiwan and never tried to go to America again. It was interesting that my two daughters studied at American universities; they left the USA like their father and grandfather. For three generations, we migrated to the richest and strongest country in the world, but we eventually gave up the opportunities offered by this great nation. I have no answer to the question 'why'. Maybe Taiwan is our home, even though we were always looking outward.

Ran Hong, CYH's grandfather, second from right at the back; Chen-Gu Hong, grandmother, centre at the front, with their 5 sons, 2 daughters and 3 grandchildren. Li-Chau Hong, CYH's father, is first from right at the back. This picture was taken in 1930s. The grandparents had 14 more grandchildren after their sons were married.

Ju-Yu Hong, CYH's mother (first from right), her parents (Mr. and Mrs. Mao-Tong Chen), younger brother and sister, taken in the 1930s.

Li-Chau Hong, CYH's father, Master of Public Health,
Johns Hopkins University, 1957.

Mei-Chen Hong, CYH's
sister, and her husband,
Tien-Chun Chang, in front
of his painting.

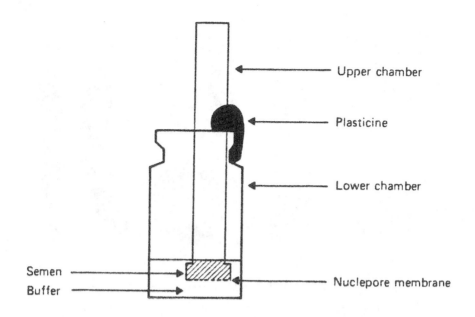

Apparatus for measuring human sperm motility
with a Trans-Membrane Migration Method invented by CYH in 1980.

The first set of Western medical books translated into Chinese by Benjamin Hobson in the
1850s. From left, Anatomy and Physiology, Natural Philosophy and Natural History,
Surgery Part One, Surgery Part Two, Midwifery and Child Diseases, Internal Medicine.
These late nineteenth century edition, traditionally thread-bound volumes are in the personal
collection of CYH.

Chinese herbal drugs studied by CYH, from left, root of Astragalus membranaceus, root of Panax notoginseng, bark of Magnolia officinalis, root of Salvia miltiorrhiza.

CYH visited Sir James Black at James Black Foundation in London, 1989.

Paul Turner visited Taiwan. Back from left: Turner, Benjamin Chiang, CYH.
Front from left: Mrs. Chiang, Mrs. Turner and Fumi Wang, 1991.

CYH (left), Fumi (right back) and two daughters visited Baruch Blumberg
at Master's Lodging, Balliol College, Oxford University, 1993.

CYH visited the nearly collapsed shrine of Hong's ancestors
at Shishi, Fukien Province, China, 2001.

Acting President's speech at commencement ceremony,
Taipei Medical University, 2008.

President's handover ceremony 2008, Taipei Medical University.
Wen-Ta Chiu (left), Tsu-Der Lee, Chairman, Board of Directors (centre), CYH (right).

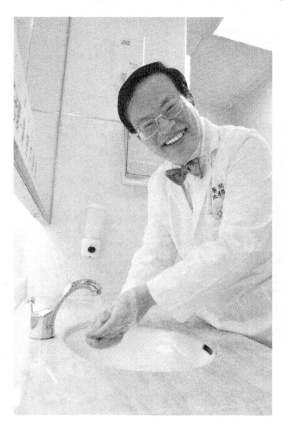

CYH promoted hand-washing
to improve patient safety at Wan
Fang Hospital,
Taipei, Taiwan, 2009.

Fumi Wang (far left) talked with Ze-Min Jiang, Chairman, People's Republic of China (second from right), at chairman's office in Beijing, 1999.

Taipei Medical University and Taipei 101 Tower,
tallest building in the world from 2004 to 2010 (left).

PART FOUR

*Exploring Chinese Medicine
and Atherosclerosis*

CHAPTER 16

Taiwan Lifts Martial Law.
The Country Moves Toward Democracy.

During my stay in Boston, the 38-year-long martial law imposed in Taiwan was lifted. Residents in Taiwan were allowed to visit their families on mainland China.

Kai-Shek Chiang, or Chiang the senior, served his position as president of the Republic in Taiwan for five eight-year terms until his death in 1975. His vice president, Chia-Kan Yen, a low-profile economist, completed his unfinished term. In 1978, Ching-Kuo Chiang, the eldest son of Chiang the senior, was elected by the National Assembly as the sixth president in 1978. He was remembered by many Taiwanese as Chiang the junior.

Members of this National Assembly enjoyed a permanent seat. Elected in 1947, they remained until the early 1990s so long as they were alive. All of them were loyal followers of Chiang the senior. In no way did they represent the citizens of Taiwan. Few in Taiwan dared to question the legitimacy of such a system. Those who did, under martial law, were sent to prison, or executed if unlucky enough to be found guilty of being a Communist.

Chiang the junior had been in power since he became the premier in 1972. He studied in Moscow when he was young, worked in factories in Siberia, became a Communist and married a Belarusian girl. Coming back to China, he worked under his father and changed into an anti-Communist. In Taiwan, his father let him take charge of intelligence agents and military forces, in addition to veterans and students' affairs. By the time his father fell ill, he was already the most powerful and feared person in Taiwan.

Even his strongest political opponents did not suspect him of corruption. His life featured simple food and thrifty dressing. He prohibited his family from getting involved in business. His senior government officers were highly capable and mostly honest in character. They made a great contribution to Taiwan's miraculous economic growth. Unlike his father who picked his staff mostly from mainlanders, he appointed many locally born Taiwanese in his cabinet. During his second term as the president, he chose Ten-Whe Lee, a Cornell-educated professor in agricultural economics, as his vice-president. Lee was born and educated in Taiwan under Japanese rule. He studied at Kyoto University but he completed his university degree in Taiwan because of the Japanese surrender. Some accused him of being a Communist when he was young. He denied, and only admitted that he read Marxist books.

In spite of his contribution to economic growth in Taiwan, Chiang the junior realized that an uprising against him and his pseudo-democratic government was approaching. Economic growth was accompanied by an urge for democracy from the people.

After ruling Taiwan with an iron fist for more than 10 years, he took a sharp turn in his policy. He became more tolerant of political demonstrations and allowed his critics to challenge political taboos. A murder accelerated his changes.

In 1984, Henry Liu, a Taiwanese American with the pen name Jiangnan, was assassinated in the garage of his house south of San Francisco, California by two gunmen from Taiwan. Liu was a vocal critic of Chiang's ruling Nationalist Party and writing an unauthorized biography of Chiang the junior. American investigators identified the two hitmen, who had already fled to Taiwan. American officers further alleged that senior intelligence officers in Taiwan orchestrated the killing of an American citizen on American soil.

Under pressure from the United States, not only the hitmen, but also several officers who were close to Chiang the junior, were sent to jail. Liu's wife filed a suit in USA against Taiwanese government; this suit was later settled out of court.

Chiang the junior openly announced that none of his sons, or any member of Chiang's family, would succeed him as president in Taiwan. The possibility of a Chiang dynasty was over. In summer 1987, he lifted martial law.

All of a sudden, a tremendous number of elderly men flew from Taiwan to China. They came with Chiang the senior from the mainland to Taiwan; during the past 40 years, they were not allowed to have any contact with family in their hometowns. Only in early 1980s, a few of them started to get messages through relatives who went abroad from China, but such correspondence had to be kept secret.

Since no direct flights were available from Taiwan to China, most of them had to change in Hong Kong. Hong Kong airport was in chaos trying to handle this sudden increase in transit passengers. It was these aged veterans' first foreign trip; they could neither follow instructions nor read signs, and they were unable to speak English or Cantonese, commonly used in Hong Kong. It was a trip that they had been waiting for; it was also long and stressful for them.

Everyone was moved to see pictures showing families reuniting. The lucky ones tearfully hugged ailing parents, middle-aged children, or the wife who had kept her promise to wait for him. Many knelt in front of the tombs of their parents, whispered for forgiveness to their re-married ex-wife, or gave souvenirs to a large group of family members whom they could hardly recognize. Stories claimed many of them gave all they had to their family and returned penniless. Like trout, some of them closed their eyes after such a trip. Even so, they regretted less than those who did not live to see the day they could go home.

Many did not know where to go; they were unable to restart any contact with their family on the mainland. All those they knew before had either passed away or left the address they remembered. Some services were provided to help them, but the information received was sometimes heartbreaking: parents or brothers executed or harassed to death. Their own flight to Taiwan may have been part of the reason for such misery.

Soon after I returned to Taipei, I reported to the hospital and started working. I was euphoric about being promoted to professor, but my boss, Benjamin Chiang, had a hard time. His family name, Chiang, sounds like that of the president's, although it is different in Chinese writing.

Benjamin took care of the president's whole family. In fact, he was also physician to many senior government officers and wealthy businessmen. He organized a special team to share his responsibility to the president. Members of this team were all colleagues at the Taipei Veterans General Hospital. Junior members of this team took it in turns to stay overnight in the president's residence when they were on duty.

Chiang the junior was in his late seventies, overweight and diabetic. His sugar control was poor, mainly because his illness did not respond to medications; he nearly lost his vision following a diabetic complication in his eyes. Neurological complications paralyzed his feet; he could not walk, he was constantly in a wheelchair and needed help to transfer him between the wheelchair and his bed. A pacemaker was inserted to keep his heart beating fast enough. He was always nauseated and retching, because of his poor stomach and intestinal peristalsis.

Benjamin had been taking care of the president since they were young. Chiang the junior had trusted Benjamin fully. Benjamin was his only senior physician; all the rest reported to Benjamin. This arrangement was quite different from Chiang the senior, who had a team of several senior physicians, one of them being Benjamin, to make decisions together. Benjamin not only treated Chiang the junior as his patient; he respected this president from his heart. He noticed that the president was compromising his health to finish the jobs in his mind; and burning the candle at both ends. In spite of his illness, the patient still had a very demanding working style.

In early 1988, the 78-year-old president suffered severe nausea, followed by massive vomiting of fresh blood from his mouth. He passed away immediately without being sent to hospital.

Since the health of the president was kept secret from the public, many people were shocked to know that Chiang the junior died suddenly. Some blamed Benjamin for not giving the president the best medical treatment. It was rumored that some government officers proposed an investigation into Benjamin's management of the president's health. It was unfair to Benjamin but he was required to keep quiet and not to defend himself.

He was given a few weeks' vacation on a Caribbean cruise after the president's funeral. On the day he returned to Taipei, I went to the airport to welcome him back. Only one colleague was present, Tsong-Ing Chen. Chen was my age; he trained in Glasgow. A handsome man with great charm, I enjoyed his jokes and always laughed loudly during our chat. We did not tell each other that either of us was going to the airport. He was a member of Benjamin's team taking care of Chiang the junior. He left VGH earlier than me to work in a hospital in central Taiwan. In our department, only three were educated in the UK: Benjamin, Chen and I.

Benjamin told me some stories about the illness of Chiang the senior.

As a soldier paying great attention to his body, he was much healthier than his son. In a traffic accident, his chest hit the front seat of his Cadillac limousine. Since then, he had had a leaky aortic valve. He then suffered from a very bad cardiac attack with severe heart failure. He was saved only after Benjamin tried a new method to dilate his blood vessels with a rarely used drug. He died after a long and protracted deterioration of his health aged 88.

Chiang the junior's successor was his vice president, Ten-Whe Lee. There were many challenges ahead for Lee. Among them was to transform Taiwan into a genuinely democratic country. His job was not easier than that of Chiang the junior; unlike the Chiangs, he never had his men in the military forces.

A group of conservatives in the Nationalist Party tried to grasp the real power and let Lee became only a figurehead. It was rumored that they sought support from Madam Kai-Shek Chiang, the step mother of Chiang the junior. Too old to engage in a tough political fight, these old guards withdrew at the last moment. Madam Chiang left Taiwan and stayed in New York until her death aged 106.

In the following years, Lee succeeded in the political transformation of Taiwan. The elder members of the legislature were forced to retire. A new parliament was organized, with all members coming from a general election. New parties were legally founded. Protests in the streets became common and accepted. There were no more restrictions on how the media should write or speak. The common practice of exchanging financial profit and business privilege for political support was exposed one by one, but did not completely disappear. Taiwan was not only one of the four Asian tigers because of its economic growth; it was also an example of how a Chinese country ruled by a totalitarian government could be changed into a democratic one without shedding blood.

CHAPTER 17

Traditional Chinese Medicine. Panax Notoginseng and the US Patent.

Traditional Chinese medicine, commonly shortened to TCM, derived its theory based on Taoism, the ancient Chinese philosophy emphasizing the harmony between human beings and nature. Health was influenced mainly by changes in environment such as temperature, season, wind and humidity etc. Drugs, exercise and acupuncture were used to correct distorted harmony. TCM was widely practised in East Asia – including China, Korea, Japan and Vietnam – before Western medicine was introduced to these countries in the 19th century.

Most drugs used in TCM were dried plants; only a small portion were derived from minerals or animals. The number of drugs has increased from 360 in the oldest pharmacopeia to thousands in the recent ones. Rainwater was a drug; soil under the feet of a hung man was a drug, too. Once a substance was listed as a drug, no one in the younger generation dared delete it, because respect to the old sages was a tradition.

Conflicts in the principle and practice of TCM were common among ancient books. TCM doctors picked up whatever they liked to rationalize their practice. The majority of medical doctors trained using modern science considered TCM to be absurd. Until recently, TCM was heavily criticized by teachers in medical schools and physicians in hospitals.

Tu, my grandfather's best friend and the earliest medical scientist in Taiwan, had a strong interest in TCM research, but all his proposals to foster such research were rejected by his colleagues, even though he taught many of them. I read his papers on TCM and believed in his foresight.

My interest in TCM was further encouraged by my mother, Fumi and Turner.

My mother was a daughter of a successful businessman selling Chinese herbal drugs in Taipei. Fumi was a pharmacist with training in pharmacognosy, the study of drugs derived from plants. Turner advised me several times that I should study TCM, both in London and during his trip to Taipei to visit me and my institute.

Jen Ku, a biology graduate, worked in my laboratory at Taipei Veterans General Hospital for years. He had extensive knowledge of TCM because several members of his family were TCM practitioners. Our first TCM project involved screening herbal extracts to assess their effects on sperm motility. With the trans-membrane migration method, we found that the commonly used tonic *Astragalus membranaceus* had a small but significant stimulatory effect. Working with colleagues in the biochemistry department, we tried to purify the active ingredient responsible for such an activity. We failed after several attempts. Our observation was published as a preliminary report with neither an identified active component nor a mechanism for the stimulatory effect.

Tonics were widely used in TCM, both for the treatment of diseases and the improvement of general health. Red ginseng from Korea, white ginseng from America and *Astragalus* from northern China were famous ones. Red ginseng was considered most potent; its common side effects included headache and sleeplessness. The other two tonics were mild in both effect and side effect; they could be prepared as a tea for a daily drink.

Disappointed by our tedious work in *Astragalus*, we shifted our interest to see if any herbal extract might improve the deformability of red blood cells. When red blood cells were moving through the capillaries, they had to change their shape from round to curved so they could be squeezed through the narrow capillary lumens without blocking them. Aged cells were fragile; they broke into fragments during their passage through the lumens. An improvement in red cell deformability might improve micro-circulation; some drugs were prescribed to patients for such a purpose. Among them the most popular one was pentoxifyllin, originally developed by Hoechst, a German drug company.

A neurologist, Shun-Sheng Chen at Kaohsiung Medical College in southern Taiwan, had an instrument made from glasses to measure the deformability of red blood cells. This instrument was a gift to his laboratory from Hoechst. I asked a skilful glass-worker to reproduce one for me. Chen studied at Queens Square Hospital for Neurological Disease in London during the early 1980s. We had maintained a friendship since we met there.

The time required for a certain amount of red blood cells to pass a Nuclepore membrane was measured as an index for the deformability of these cells. Cells with better deformability passed very quickly, while the worst one took longer. A drug that shortened the passage time was considered to improve deformability. It was interesting that Nuclepore membrane was twice an important component in my research. In London, I used it to measure sperm motility.

Our experiment showed that extract of *Panax notoginseng* was found to improve red cell deformability. *Panax notoginseng* was classified in TCM as a drug for activating blood circulation and dissolving stasis. It was widely used externally for the treatment of cut injuries. Some TCM doctors recommended it for stopping internal hemorrhages such as gastrointestinal bleeding. There was no modern research to prove or disprove any of these effects.

With the assistance of Sheau-Farn Yeh, a female professor of biochemistry, we tested different fractions of this herbal extract to purify the active ingredient from it. To our great surprise, the most active one was trilinolein, a lipid.

Many naturally occurring lipids were triglycerides; they were made from a glycerol backbone attached to three fatty acids. These fatty acids varied in type. Animal fats, solid at room temperature, contained more saturated fatty acids so they were rigid and more likely to induce atherosclerosis. Vegetable fats, liquid at room temperature, contained more unsaturated fatty acids, which were more flexible and healthy.

The three fatty acids in trilinolein were all unsaturated linoleic acid. Trilinolein was a chemical known to be present in some seed oils.

We conducted a series of experiments on trilinolein. It suppressed platelet aggregation and adhesion of white blood cells to the inner layer of the artery. It also induced relaxation of arteries and reduced the necrotic area of the heart muscle when a rat coronary artery was ligated. All these findings supported a beneficial effect of trilinolein in the treatment of cardiac attack.

We applied for a Taiwanese and a US patent for developing trilinolein into a drug. It was a new challenge for me. There was no one in the hospital or medical school who could help me to deal with issues of intellectual property. I had to go through the processes with my own efforts and pocket money. Answering the questions raised by patent examiners was frustrating. Patent lawyers were very expensive, but essential. We spent three years getting our US patent approved in 1996. A Taiwanese patent was granted after I informed the patent office that a US patent had been issued to us.

Many scientists, including my younger self, believed that a patent was key to getting rich. The reality was that very few patents had commercial value and a successful product needed several patents for coverage. Before it expired, our patent on trilinolein had not been transferred to any company and we did not earn a penny from it. I continued to pay an annual maintenance fee to the patent offices. Few drug companies were willing to develop a known compound into a new drug. A use patent was not as protective as a patent on a brand new chemical. For trilinolein, we only held a use patent, not a chemical patent.

Our studies on *Panax notoginseng* did not answer the question of why this herb was widely used in TCM to stop bleeding and repair cut wounds. We did not prove that it prevented a heart attack when patients took it orally. More research was required for these unsolved questions.

Returning from Boston to Taipei, I continued to work as a cardiologist at the Veterans General Hospital. I also joined a new Institute of Clinical Medicine at Yang-Ming Medical College. This institute enrolled medical doctors who completed their clinical training, taught them research methods and granted them a PhD when they completed a thesis. The purpose of this institute was simple: to cultivate more physician-scientists like me. The director of this institute was Benjamin Chiang.

I took part in hiring faculty members and selecting students for the new institute. Benjamin and I picked students based on their previous academic performance, regardless of which medical school they had graduated from or in what hospital they received their resident training. I designed the curriculum for this new institute based on my experience in London.

Students' backgrounds varied. They came from different clinical departments; research training had to be tailored to their individual career planning. Because I had been working with several researchers on campus, I helped each student to find a suitable advisor to learn laboratory techniques. We were not training these students to become basic scientists, but we encouraged them to refresh their knowledge of basic medicine and apply it to clinical research. Discussion with these bright and strongly motivated students during seminar sessions updated my understanding of many specialties in medicine; I enjoyed such an intellectual exercise.

It was indeed my privilege as a newly appointed professor to participate in the founding stage of an institute that turned out to be the most important and productive one at Yang-Ming. Its contribution to the transformation of Taipei Veterans General Hospital from a service oriented hospital to a research medical centre was well recognized.

CHAPTER 18

Institute of Traditional Medicine. Magnolol and Salvianolic Acid.

I n 1991, an Institute of Traditional Medicine was founded at Yang-Ming Medical College; the next year I was invited to be the director of this institute.

Its first director was Professor Julia J. Tsuei. This institute was indeed her baby; it was only through her enthusiasm and idealism that it could be founded. Tsuei completed her clinical training in obstetrics and gynecology in the United States and came back to Taiwan as chief of the Maternal and Child Centre at Taipei Veterans General Hospital, where she pioneered family planning during the 1970s. She had a strong interest in acupuncture and constantly promoted the interchange between TCM practitioners and mainstream doctors.

When this institute opened, she was 64 – just one year before the age of compulsory retirement in a public school. Shou-Hwa Han, Dean of the college, asked me if I would take the directorship of this institute.

I was surprised by this invitation and my first reaction was 'no'. The Institute of Clinical Medicine where I was serving as a professor was much more established; it was a PhD program supported by the hospital and rich in resources. I was well respected there as a deputy to Benjamin Chiang.

On the other hand, the Institute of Traditional Medicine provided only a master level of education; its laboratory was rudimentary and its budget minimal. Most, if not all, my colleagues still considered research into TCM a dubious endeavor.

With the encouragement of Turner, Fumi and my mother, I looked at this job from a different point of view. TCM was becoming more and more popular internationally. Unlike the Institute of Clinical Medicine where students and faculty members came from different medical disciplines, research at the Institute of Traditional Medicine could be more focused. As a director, I could lead the team to a few topics that I considered important and interesting.

In summer 1992, I took the new position. A small room on the top floor of the library was my temporary office. Students scattered around different laboratories on campus; they were young, most of them medical or pharmacy graduates from the China Medical College in central Taiwan where undergraduate teaching in TCM was provided.

I was very lucky to find two young MD-PhDs to join this new institute.

Yi-Tsau Huang was a medical graduate of Yang-Ming. Like me, he received a government scholarship for studying abroad. I wrote a recommendation letter for him to apply to a British university. In Glasgow he completed his PhD in clinical pharmacology. To improve his knowledge in TCM, he attended a one-and-a-half-year weekend course in TCM at China Medical College. Herbal treatment for portal hypertension in liver failure was his major research interest.

Jen-Hwe Chiu was a surgeon. He got his PhD at the Institute of Clinical Medicine at Yang-Ming. Determined to apply his knowledge in clinical surgery and molecular biology to scientific research into herbal drugs and acupuncture, he spent a few months in China learning acupuncture on animals so that his future research on acupuncture could be free from the interference of human factors. He went to Tibet nearly every year; he had a very good knowledge of Tibetan medicine which was strongly influenced by traditional Indian medicine.

We three were all MD-PhDs with solid training in both Western medicine and modern science. We were not TCM practitioners; progress in TCM brought no financial benefit to us. We shared an ideal that TCM was worthy of serious investigation, no matter how others judged it. There was a vision in our mind that someday this institute would be an internationally recognized stronghold for TCM research. None of us regretted the choice we had made at that moment.

When a new building was completed on campus, we had more space for offices, classrooms and laboratories. After I stepped down, Huang succeeded me as the director; he later moved from Yang-Ming to become the director of a National Research Institute of Chinese Medicine and Chiu succeeded his position at Yang Ming.

My own research at this institute began with mitochondria, a cellular organelle that served as a power plant for supplying energy in the cell. Since both sperm and the heart were moving constantly, energy supply from mitochondria to these cells was vital for them to function normally.

Yau-Huei Wei, professor of biochemistry, was an expert in mitochondria. Originally an agricultural chemist, he obtained a PhD from the State University of New York in Rochester. We had co-operated on several research projects since I came back from London. Wei was skilful in explaining complicated biochemical mechanisms in simple and understandable language; besides, he was always inspiring and innovative in his research. A true educator and scientist, he was appointed as the founding Dean for the newly established Mackay Medical College, affiliated with the historic Mackay Memorial Hospital, in 2009.

One of his PhD students tried to study some specific mitochondrial enzyme in sperm. The volume of human semen per ejaculation ranges from 3ml-5ml – it was too little for this student to prepare an adequate amount of spermatic enzyme. He asked a female technician at the College of Agriculture, Taiwan University to collect pig semen for him. It turned out that a 400kg boar produced around 400ml of semen for each ejaculation – that was too much for him to handle. She changed the donor to a 60Kg mini-pig, which produced around 60ml of semen per ejaculation. Pigs' ejaculation was proportional: 1ml to 1kg body weight; no wonder pigs are a symbol of fertility in China. We shared interesting information such as this during our research meetings. Our research was full of fun; we all enjoyed it.

Most of the time, Wei used liver mitochondria for his research since it was easy to prepare. I asked him if we could purify mitochondria from cardiac cells. It could be difficult, he answered, because mitochondria in the heart was tightly packed between muscle fibers. Based on techniques learned from Wei, it took a year for an assistant of mine to isolate mitochondria from rat hearts.

Under my supervision, a graduate student screened the effect of Chinese herbal drugs on mitochondria. This time, we tested compounds purified from herbs, rather than crude extracts of them. We did not want to repeat the tedious work of isolation, purification and identification if an activity was discovered in one of the herbs. Thousands of chemicals have been purified from medicinal herbs; some of those I tested were purchased from chemical companies, while others were gifts from colleagues interested in TCM.

We found that magnolol and honokiol, two compounds with similar chemical structure purified from *Magnolia officinalis*, were very potent in inhibiting lipid peroxidation on mitochondria. They were a thousand times more potent as an antioxidant than vitamin E, a reference standard for antioxidant activity.

Cells constantly produce free radicals. Excessive production or accumulation of them induces lipid peroxidation, which was considered crucial in the pathogenesis of cellular damage leading to cancer, atherosclerosis and degenerative diseases. Antioxidants were chemicals that scavenged free radicals and prevented a chain reaction of lipid peroxidation in the cell. Foods rich in antioxidants had been widely promoted as healthy supplements, but there was still a lack of clinical trials that demonstrated any antioxidant as a drug in preventing or treating human diseases.

Plants classified into the *magnolia* genus were widely distributed around the world. *Magnolia officinalis* was a specific type of *magnolia*. Its bark was used in TCM for the treatment of abdominal fullness or chest tightness, commonly considered to be disturbed circulation of 'Qi' in the body. Qi was a basic concept in TCM, roughly equivalent to 'vitality' in the modern sense. Magnolol and honokiol were isolated more than half a century ago and previous investigators found they have an anti-microbial effect.

We published our results in *Biochemical Pharmacology*. It was the most quoted paper of mine; around 200 scientists referenced it in their publications. My colleagues and I tested other chemicals purified from Chinese herbal drugs in our subsequent experiments; none of them were more potent than magnolol and honokiol. With animal studies, we demonstrated their effects in protecting the heart, sperm and liver against free radical-induced damage. Recently, these two chemicals were intensively studied for their anti-cancer effect, particularly in China and the USA.

Another graduate student of mine induced atherosclerosis to rabbits by feeding them a fat-rich diet. Rabbits given a water extract of *Salvia miltiorrhiza* were found to have a lesser degree of atherosclerosis. Lipid levels in their blood were comparable to those not treated with the extract. We analyzed the chemical compounds in the extract and found it to be rich in Salvianolic acid.

We concluded that a Salvianolic acid-rich extract of the herb was an effective drug to prevent atherosclerosis, without lowering blood lipid level. This paper was published in *Arteriosclerosis, Thrombosis and Vascular Biology*, one of the leading international journals in atherosclerosis research. Very few papers on TCM had ever been published there. We did not even test a pure chemical compound, which was commonly required for a high quality research.

Salvia miltiorrhiza, or danshen in Chinese, was one of the most widely used Chinese herbal drugs for the treatment of cardiovascular diseases such as coronary atherosclerosis with angina chest pain. Sometimes called dark red ginseng, its application was in fact quite different from ginseng, which was a popular tonic.

There were many papers published by scientists in China on the anti-platelet and protective cardiovascular effects of Tanshinon, a lipid-soluble component isolated from *Salvia miltiorrhiza*. We were the first team to demonstrate the therapeutic potential of its water-soluble part in cardiovascular diseases. Tanshison was small in its chemical structure so it was easier to synthesize; salvianolic acid, on the other hand, was a much bigger and more complicated chemical.

My studies on trilinolein from *Panax notoginseng*, magnolol from *Magnolia officinalis* and salvianolic acid from *Salvia miltiorrhiza* brought my research career to another peak. I was frequently invited to talk or write on the cardiovascular effects of TCM and the antioxidant activities of Chinese herbal drugs, both in Taiwan and abroad. I succeeded in transforming my research from sperm function to cardiovascular medicine.

With effort from all my faculty staff and students, the Institute of Traditional Medicine rapidly became a productive and respected unit at Yang-Ming. I was invited to sit on the Committee for Chinese Medicine and Pharmacy at the Ministry of Health. All other medical doctors on this committee were TCM practitioners; I was the only exception. The Society of Chinese Natural Medicine also elected me as its president; most members in this society were active Taiwanese researchers in pharmacy or pharmacological departments.

Looking back, my accomplishment in TCM research was limited – none of my findings resulted in a change of patient management. What I demonstrated to others was the future potential of TCM. I was one of the first medical doctors outside mainland China to engage in a serious scientific investigation of TCM. My vision was the integration of TCM into mainstream medicine. In 2013, my alma mater medical school bestowed on me a chair professorship in integrative medicine to support my efforts in this undertaking. It was my last title before retirement.

In 1994, Yang-Ming Medical College was granted university status by the Ministry of Education in Taiwan. Several medical colleges, including my alma mater, were likewise promoted in the following years. TCM research is now popular in every medical university in Taiwan, not only Yang-Ming. As an admirer of Tsung-Ming Tu, my grandfather's best friend, I followed Tu's steps in pharmacological research (in which he made great achievements); additionally I contributed to the modernization of TCM, which had been an unfulfilled dream of Tu's.

CHAPTER 19

Chinese Medical Scientists.
West Lake, a Paradise on Earth.

Being the director of the Institute of Traditional Medicine, I had several opportunities to interact with Chinese medical scientists. Before that, Fumi and I made a private visit to Beijing in August 1990.

We flew from Hong Kong to the Capital Airport. We did not know anyone in Beijing, so arranged the trip and travelled all on our own.

After checking in at the hotel, we could not wait to take a taxi to see this great city. We first visited the Temple of Heaven, which Chinese emperors from the 15th century onwards visited annually and where they prayed to heaven for a good harvest. Its blue roof was beautiful and mysterious. Over the following five days, we visited the Forbidden City, Great Wall, Tiananmen Square, the Summer Palace and several museums. All of them were impressively unique and huge in size.

One year before our visit, a student demonstration at Tiananmen Square had been suppressed with tanks; many foreigners withdrew their investment in China and the number of tourists fell sharply. One month after our visit, an Asian Olympics would be held in Beijing; the Chinese were trying to improve their international image by showing their best to their guests. Flowers flourished along the boulevards; the outer walls of big buildings were cleaned and colorful flags flew all over the city.

Restaurant food was disappointing and goods in shops were unattractive. People dressed simply; not many cars were running in the streets. A Bank of China Foreign Exchange Certificate, not the ordinary Renminbi used by

Chinese, was the currency for tourists. In the famous Quanjude Roast Duck Restaurant, we had to queue and buy a ticket for our dishes before finding a seat and starting to eat.

There was an air of tranquility and elegance to the capital. It was royal, even though the emperor had gone forever. We loved this city; its characters could never be found in any other part of the world. Rich in culture and heritage, it was a symbol of China.

In the early 1990s, Yang-Ming started to host visiting scholars from China. Chi-Shen Han was the first Chinese medical scientist to visit Taiwan since both sides of Taiwan Strait had attempted to reconcile.

Han was a professor at Beijing Medical University, which was later merged into Beijing University as its medical college. He discovered that levels of endorphins in the brain increased when one received acupuncture treatment. Endorphins were regarded as endogenous morphine that relieved the sensation of pain. Han's finding explained why acupuncture could be used for pain relief. He was well known internationally as a top-notch physiologist and neuroscientist. Most interestingly, he was a classmate of Benjamin Chiang's at high school. After not seeing each other for almost half a century, they happily reunited.

In 1992, a delegate team from Yang-Ming Medical College officially visited leading medical institutions in China. Benjamin Chiang and I were part of it. Three other members of the team were Han, Dean of Yang-Ming, Tsuei, founder of the Institute of Traditional Medicine, and Wei-Kung Wang, a Johns Hopkins-educated biophysicist with a long interest in Qigong. Qigong, sometimes interchangeable with Tai-Chi, was a slow-paced physical exercise practiced by the Chinese to improve health; it was based on the theory of TCM. Visitors to China were often surprised to see many men and women practicing Qigong in the parks every morning. A paper published in the *New England Journal of Medicine* in 2012 showed that patients with Parkinson's disease had better posture, fewer falls and improved walking ability after practicing Tai-Chi. Tai-Chi was becoming more and more popular outside China.

Leaders at Beijing Medical University, Peking Union Medical College, the Chinese Academy of Medical Sciences and China Academy of Traditional Chinese Medicine welcomed us sincerely and showed us their best research.

We met Keji Chen, an academician at the Chinese Academy of Sciences.

He was the leader of integrative Chinese and Western medicine in China. Originally a doctor of Western medicine, he learned TCM in the 1950s when Mao promoted TCM and asked Western-style medical doctors to integrate TCM into their practice.

Chen guided us to see how his patients were diagnosed and treated with both TCM and modern Western medicine. His researches on *Salvia miltiorrhiza* and other Chinese herbal drugs in cardiovascular diseases were most interesting to me. From our first meeting, we developed a long friendship. I was his host in Taipei during his first visit to Taiwan in 1993; one of his students came to Yang-Ming to complete parts of her experiment for a doctoral thesis. He invited me to sit in the editorial board of the *Chinese Journal of Integrated Traditional and Western Medicine*, both Chinese and English editions. He was editor-in-chief of these two journals. When *People's Daily*, the official newspaper of the Chinese government, interviewed him about his first trip to Taiwan, he gave them a picture taken with me at Taipei Veterans General Hospital. My name and face appeared in *People's Daily*, not common for a Taiwanese.

At the China Academy of Traditional Chinese Medicine, which was later named the China Academy of Chinese Medical Sciences, we were introduced to You-You Tu, a female scientist who led a team that discovered artemisinin for the treatment of malaria, derived from a Chinese medicinal herb, *Artemisia annula* or Qinghao in Chinese. Major parts of this work were done during the Vietnam War, when she and her colleagues were asked to study anti-malarial drugs for the assistance of the malaria-ridden army in tropical jungles.

Artermisinin was most useful to treat strains of malaria resistant to classical drugs such as quinidine. It was advised that artermisinin be combined with other anti-malarial drugs, rather than used as a mono-therapy so as to avoid the emergence of a drug-resistant strain of the malaria parasite. Some scientists were trying to modify its chemical structure and produce more potent derivatives. Such derivatives would not have made a big profit, because most patients suffering from malaria were living in poor, developing countries. In 2011, she was given a Lasker Award from the United States. This award was considered to be the highest achievement in medicine given by America.

We also visited Chongqing, Wuhan and Shanghai in western, central and eastern China respectively. We met senior faculty members in the best medical schools and hospitals there. On our way from Chongqing to Wuhan, we took a ship sailing down-stream along the Yangtze Gorge. We stopped over in a town where the 18 stories of hell below the earth were shown. Buildings and figures in this interesting amusement park were based on ancient Chinese mythology.

When the official programs finished at Shanghai, Fumi flew to join me; then we accompanied Benjamin Chiang and his wife to Hangzhou 180km south of Shanghai. Hangzhou was the capital city of Zhejiang Province, where Benjamin was born. He spent many years in Hangzhou with his parents when he was young. After he left China, he never returned to Hangzhou to see his parents and siblings. This was the first time in 50 years he had returned and visited the tombs of his parents.

We stayed at the Shangri-La Hotel near the West Lake. Soon after we arrived, Fumi and I walked along the nearby Su-Di Causeway, and watched a beautiful sunset. This causeway, with willow trees along the banks, was built by Dong-Po Su in the 11th century. He was a great statesman, artist and poet. When he served as a governor of this city, he built this bank famous for its trees, flowers, bridges and lake view.

During the next 20 years, I flew to China around 100 times. I travelled extensively in China, visiting most if not all of the well-known attractions in this country. Among them, Hangzhou, its West Lake in particular, was my favorite. No wonder that the ancient Chinese called it a paradise on earth. Its beauty was described as intoxicating.

I once spent six hours walking slowly for 15km around the lake. It was a cold winter day, snowing in the morning; not many people appeared. The lake showed me its beauty in silence.

In a morning, the whole lake was covered with a thick fog. I stood on the lakeside; a small ship suddenly came out from the fog. Soon it disappeared quietly into the fog. Not a trace was left; I wondered if it was a dream. Very quickly the sunshine appeared; the sky immediately cleared, blue water and green hills reached as far as I could see. The lake showed me its charm in these changes.

One evening, I passed by the Broken Bridge where, according to legend, a scholar met a lady who was transformed from a white snake. A fortune teller told me that Buddha was in my heart, there was no need to search for him from outside. I was enlightened to learn this lesson.

There was a 1,000-year-old Baopu Taoist Temple on the hills of the northern shore of the lake. I climbed the stone steps to reach it. Bao Puzi, also known as Ge Hong, who was a Taoist priest during the fourth century, tried to make immortality pills here. He wrote a medical book entitled *Handbook of Prescriptions for Emergencies*, in which Qinghao was listed as a herbal drug for the treatment of malaria, or 'intermittent fever' as the disease was known at that time. You-You Tu and her colleagues read that book and purified artemisinin from that herb.

On the yellowish wall of the temple, there were four large Chinese characters which said 'hold the simple and guard the true'. I suddenly realized that in the temple of an alchemist who was supposed to make a miracle drug for an eternal life, the most important teaching was to have a mind that was simple and to keep a life that was true.

On the west shore of the lake there was a hotel named Xihu State Guesthouse. It was formerly a Liu Village. Nixon met Mao in a lakeside villa of the hotel during his historic ice-breaking visit to China. This hotel, located in a corner not convenient for tourists, enjoyed one of the best views of West Lake. It was a favorite resort for Mao when he was staying in Hangzhou. Certainly it was also my favorite.

On the south side, there was a Leifeng Pagoda. The original brick tower built in AD 975 fell in 1924; the new one was constructed in 2002. Visitors could enjoy a magnificent panoramic view of the lake from the top of this tower.

The number of tourists visiting West Lake was increasing year by year. Its utmost beauty and tranquility could not be so well appreciated among the crowds. That was the price paid for economic growth.

There were many museums in Hangzhou. Among them, I was most interested in a traditional Chinese medicine museum. It was attached to a Hu Qing Yu Tang Herbal Drugstore founded by Xue-Yan Hu. Hu was a wealthy businessman in the 19th century. He started as a banker; his business involved salt, tea, silk, and grain as well as the arms trade. He did not have training in medicine, but he opened a drug store claiming that his shop supplied only herbs of the best quality. He was bankrupted before he died but this drugstore developed into a significant pharmaceutical company.

Hu's formal residence in downtown Hangzhou was also a museum. Visiting this luxurious mansion, one could get an impression of how one of the richest men in the Qing dynasty lived. Both the traditional Chinese medicine museum and his residence were good examples of the beauty of architectural style in southern China.

After dark, one could watch a grand outdoor show of lights, music, dance and theatrics upon the lake. Yi-Mou Zhang, the Chinese movie director who developed the opening and closing ceremonies of the 2008 Beijing Olympics, produced a performance called *Impression West Lake*. The beauty and myths of the lake, as well as the culture and folklore of the city, were vividly presented in this spectacular open-air show.

Beijing is the capital of China, its political centre for more than eight centuries. It shows the grandiosity of an ancient empire. Shanghai is a business centre developed from a small country town by Westerners in less than 200 years. It shows the power of wealth. Hangzhou is the soul of the Chinese, a dream of poets and artists. It shows the sophistication of a delicate culture.

CHAPTER 20

Lipids and Atherosclerosis. Blumberg and Sir John Vane.

Besides TCM, during the early 1990s I was involved in a project about lipid-lowering drugs. Elevated levels of cholesterol, along with hypertension, diabetes and smoking were the most important risk factors for atherosclerosis and its complications such as stroke, myocardial infarction and peripheral artery diseases.

Michael Brown and Joseph Goldstein, two American physician-scientists working at the University of Texas Southwestern Medical Centre in Dallas discovered how cholesterol was regulated in the body, why serum cholesterol was elevated and which drugs could be used for the treatment of hypercholesterolemia. They were awarded a Nobel Prize in Medicine in 1985.

During the early 1970s, Akira Endo, a scientist working for the Japanese drug company Sankyo, discovered from a fungus a drug that suppressed the synthesis of cholesterol in the body. It was the first of a new class of drugs named HMG-CoA reductase inhibitors, since they all inhibited an enzyme in liver call HMG-CoA reductases. This medical term was too long to spell; they were often called statins because every drug of this class had a name that ended with statin. Sankyo's drug, pravastatin, was marked under the brand name Mevalotin in Eastern Asia and Pravachol in USA or Europe, while Merck's lovastatin was marketed globally with the brand name Mevacor.

When Sankyo and Merck were starting to sell their statins in Taiwan, they asked Benjamin Chiang to test these drugs on patients. Until then, these drugs had never been tried among Chinese. Benjamin assigned this job to me. We gave pravastatin and lovastatin to two groups of patients for three months. The results were remarkable. These drugs were effective and well-tolerated, better than any other lipid-lowering drug we had known before. In addition to the change in serum cholesterol, which was a common indicator of serum lipid disorder, we measured the fatty acid profile in the lipoprotein of these patients.

Other drug companies developed their own statins; most of them were more potent than pravastatin and lovastatin. Currently, atrovastatin (marketed by Pfizer under the brand name Lipitor) is the best-selling drug in the world, with a peak sale of US$9bn dollars a year.

I was invited to many medical conferences, both domestic and international, to talk about the use of statins in the treatment of elevated cholesterol. Selling statins became one of the most important businesses for multinational drug companies. They sponsored the speakers and participants attending these medical meetings. I became less and less interested in these promotional activities and eventually withdrew from all of them.

The profit-driven drug companies and some medical doctors sponsored by them were criticized by the *British Medical Journal* in its editorial comments against 'Too Much Medicine'.

Drug companies could enjoy patent protection once they developed a new drug. Very often, the new drug was only marginally better than the old ones. Since the old ones were off-patent and less profitable, the drug companies promoted the new and expensive one as if it was a breakthrough. Older ones were sold as generic drugs at a cheaper price. Most budget-conscientious insurance agents suggested medical doctors prescribe generic drugs to their patients. I supported this policy, as long as the quality of the generic ones was strictly controlled.

Drug companies also tried to persuade medical doctors to give drugs to as many patients as possible. One of their strategies was to lower the threshold for the indication of a drug. A good example was mildly elevated blood pressure. It was known that complications in hypertension increased in proportion to blood pressure levels. However, repeated clinical trials had failed to demonstrate a reduction in complications or death rate if the drug was given to patients with mild hypertension but no associated diseases. Attempts to persuade normal subjects to lower their blood pressure below

130 or even 120 in order to expand the market for anti-hypertensive drugs were denied in treatment guidelines published by impartial organizations such as the UK's National Institute of Clinical Excellence.

In other diseases such as diabetes and lipid disorders, some over-enthusiastic experts were trying to label mildly elevated sugar or cholesterol levels as abnormal and advising more healthy subjects to take drugs. Since the risk for cardiovascular or other complications in this group of people was very low, the majority of drugs prescribed to them were wasted. Only drug companies reaped a huge profit from such a practice.

Many diseases are invented by people selling remedies for these diseases. Modern people live with a constant worry about their health because they are bombarded by overwhelming threats that they need drugs to keep healthy. Selling prevention becomes a better business than treating diseases. Aldous Huxley, author of *Brave New World*, said 'Medical science has made such tremendous progress there is hardly a healthy human left'.

Drug treatment should be individualized. New and potent statins are suitable only for patients with signs or symptoms of atherosclerosis and are refractory to commonly used statins. Elevated cholesterol in most patients could be managed with simple and cheap generic statins. Highly potent statins were known to carry an increased risk of diabetes. I would not recommend aggressive drug treatment for healthy subjects with borderline cholesterol levels. Body weight reduction by diet control and regular exercise is their first choice.

Benjamin Chiang established the Taiwan Society of Lipid and Atherosclerosis and acted as its first president. I succeeded him as the second one. Whenever possible, I resisted the pressure of drug companies to push the sale of their new and expensive statins. The same principle should be applied to other categories of drugs.

Not being a specialist in liver or infectious diseases, I became unexpectedly involved in a study of hepatitis because of my interest in herbal drugs.

One day in 1988, Shou-Dong Lee, chief of gastroenterology at Taipei Veterans General Hospital, gave me a telephone call asking me if I would be interested in an Indian herb *Phyllanthus amarus*. He had just read a paper in *The Lancet* reporting a beneficial effect of this herb in the treatment of hepatitis B. Baruch Blumberg, the 1976 Nobel laureate in medicine for his discovery of the hepatitis B virus, worked with some Indian scientists to undertake the clinical trial in India. Before starting their study on patients, they tested the herb on woodchucks that carried a hepatitis virus and found it effective.

Hepatitis B was rife among Chinese. Infected mothers transmitted the virus to their newborn babies through blood contamination during delivery. This type of infection was called a vertical transmission. More than 10% of Chinese carried the hepatitis virus in their liver because of this. In Europe or America, most patients were infected after they had reached adulthood by either blood transfusion or shared needles.

In Taiwan, since the 1980s, when blood testing to detect the virus and a vaccine to prevent it both became available, every baby born to mothers carrying the virus has been vaccinated to prevent being infected. Taiwan was one of the first countries to implement a nationwide hepatitis B vaccination program, which not only reduced hepatitis infection but also led to a marked reduction in liver cancer. However, up until the time Blumberg and his Indian colleagues published their paper in *The Lancet*, there was no treatment for patients who had already been infected with the virus. Many of them would die of liver cirrhosis or liver cancer.

Blumberg was a New Yorker. He studied medicine at Columbia University and then went to Oxford to obtain a PhD in biochemistry. During his study of serum proteins at the National Institute of Health in Bethesda, Maryland, he isolated an unusual antigen from the blood of an Australian aborigine. His persistent efforts in researching the origin of this abnormality resulted in the identification of it as a marker for hepatitis B infection. This antigen was in fact a fragment of the viral protein.

I tried to get some dried *Phyllanthus amarus* from India. An Indian banker helped me to collect it. He advertised in an English paper in India, asking for anyone who could provide such a herb. Tsu-Der Lee, my former colleague at Taipei Medical College Hospital, knew the son of the banker and introduced him to me. Lee and I flew to New Delhi, India to arrange the transport of these herbs. We asked Professor Grady Webster at University of California in Davis, who identified the plant for the clinical trial in India, if the herb we collected was the same as that tested by Blumberg's colleagues; he confirmed that we had the right one.

One of my colleagues at Yang-Ming had a liver cell line to which a gene of hepatitis virus was transfected. We tested the effect of this herb on the production of viral antigen in the cultured cells. It did suppress viral antigen production and we proposed a molecular mechanism for this suppression. However, like the stimulatory effect of *Astragalus* on sperm motility, we were unable to isolate the active component of Phyllanthus that suppressed viral activity. We published a paper to report our findings.

By the early 2000s, there were several anti-viral drugs developed for the treatment of hepatitis B. *Phyllanthus* was put aside, no matter if it worked or not.

My research on *Phyllanthus* was not as successful as I expected; however, I was able to develop a personal friendship with Blumberg because of this work. In 1993, Fumi and I took our two daughters on our first family trip to England. Before we left Taipei, I sent my paper on *Phyllanthus* to Blumberg who at that time was the master of Balliol College in Oxford. I asked him if my family and I could visit him in Oxford.

He was very kind and arranged afternoon tea with us at the master's lodgings. Afterwards, he came to Taiwan several times. Despite his busy schedule, he found time to have dinner with Fumi and me, and went sightseeing with us in Taipei. He refused to take a traditional Taiwanese dish prepared from clams. 'It would be a joke if I get hepatitis after taking it,' he told us. Hepatitis A, not B, could be transmitted through contaminated clams.

Blumberg worked at the Fox Chase Cancer Centre at Philadelphia, Pennsylvania after he returned from Oxford to the USA. He died in 2011 aged 85. He was a great man who saved millions of patients; his research terminated forever the vertical transmission of this fatal disease among Chinese. What Fumi and I remembered most was his friendly personality and his infectious curiosity.

Professors who had served for more than seven years at Yang-Ming could take sabbatical leave of up to one year. During this year, the professor could stay in some host institute, reading, writing, or doing research there; his salary would be paid as usual and his obligation in teaching would be waived. This was a system for senior faculty members to keep up-to-date. However, most members of clinical faculties did not enjoy this privilege because of their responsibility to patients in the hospital.

In 1996, I had been serving as a professor for nearly 10 years. I applied for a six-month sabbatical. After correspondence with several foreign institutes, I chose to spend three months in the Centre for East-West Medicine at the University of California, Los Angeles and three months in the William Harvey Research Institute at St. Bartholomew's Hospital Medical College, London.

First I went to Los Angeles. Ka Kit Hui at the Centre for East-West Medicine was my host. He taught students traditional Chinese medicine (TCM) at the medical school and ran a clinic in Santa Monica Boulevard where he gave TCM treatment to patients. Many patients with chronic pain refracted by conventional therapies came a long way to see him; his treatments were mainly based on the theory of acupuncture. Like me, he was a medical doctor trained in internal medicine and clinical pharmacology before shifting his interest to TCM. He was a pioneer among American doctors who tried to develop TCM in the setting of an academic medical centre.

Now, TCM in the USA is covered under the more inclusive term 'complementary and alternative medicine' or CAM in short. It is taught in many American medical schools and its services are provided by a large number of American hospitals.

Fumi and I took a bus tour from Los Angeles to Yellow Stone. On the way, we stopped over in several national parks. The wild west of America was magnificent and beautiful.

While we were in Los Angeles, there was a crisis in the Taiwan Strait. Ten-Whe Lee, who succeeded Chiang the junior as president of Taiwan, gradually moved his government away from the one-China policy. During the past decades, this policy had been recognized by both mainland China and Taiwan. When he was running for a second presidential term in Taiwan's first ever direct election, China warned that if anyone declared Taiwanese independence, China would use military force against Taiwan. In all previous elections, including Lee's first term, the president had been chosen in a ballot of National Assembly members.

Shortly before the election, the Chinese army fired several sets of missiles to the sea off Keelung and Kaohsiung, major seaports in Taiwan. It was obviously intended to discourage Taiwanese from supporting Lee. Americans sent a naval fleet, led by two air carriers, to patrol in the open sea surrounding Taiwan. Lee won a majority of the votes and continued his presidency for four more years.

The second part of my sabbatical leave was spent in London. In 1985, Sir John Vane established the William Harvey Research Institute at the medical school of St. Bartholomew's Hospital. Located in the Charterhouse

Square close to the hospital, this institute soon became a world-leading pharmacological centre devoted to therapeutic innovation in cardiovascular and inflammatory diseases.

Vane studied the anti-platelet effect of aspirin. The wide use of aspirin in preventing strokes and myocardial infarction was a clinical application of his findings. He shared the Nobel Prize in Medicine with Sune Bergstrom and Bengt Samuelsson of Sweden for their research into prostaglandins in 1982. Prostaglandins were part of the mechanism of aspirin and Vane's work led to a full understanding of their interrelationship.

I was very happy to return to Barts, except that Turner had died two years previously. He suffered from coronary artery disease, myocardial infarction and arrhythmia in his later life. During the Christmas service at a church near his house in Ascot, he died suddenly in the presence of his family and friends. He was buried in the graveyard of that church.

One day in London, I received a telephone from Taipei asking me if I would like to take the position as Dean of Academic Affairs at Yang-Ming.

Yang-Ming Medical College was upgraded to Yang-Ming University in 1994. Luke S. Chang, chief of surgery at Taipei Veterans General Hospital, was elected to succeed Han as president in 1996. Chang was familiar with my researches on sperm since he specialized in urology. He also knew my work at the Institute of Clinical Medicine, where several of his junior staff studied for their doctoral degree. I accepted his invitation and shortened my stay in London. Before leaving the UK, Fumi and I took a bus tour visiting Stonehenge, Leeds, Bath, York, Edinburgh, the Lake District, and Liverpool etc. It was a journey we had wanted to take for a long time.

PART FIVE

*Experiencing Management in Business
and University*

CHAPTER 21

Educating the Next Generation.
Fumi's Companies and Artemisinin.

took the new position as a Dean of Academic Affairs at Yang-Ming University in August, 1996. The campus was empty and most students and teachers were away for their summer vacations. On the first day Chang and I took office we were told a medical student had died in a traffic accident on his way back from volunteering in the countryside. On behalf of the university, I immediately took a train to his home in southern Taiwan and attended his funeral. That was the first assignment of my Deanship.

Chang was a capable surgeon. He invented a computer-assisted instrument for removing prostate tissue during operations for prostate hypertrophy. One of the risks of such a procedure was the accidental perforation of the outer prostate capsule. By sensing the difference between the densities of the glandular tissue and the capsule, this instrument would automatically cut off the power supply once the capsule was touched. He got a US patent and transferred the technology to a foreign company that specialized in producing surgical instruments. All income from the patent was donated to a foundation for urological research. The company paid him only a small up-front fee but never developed his invention into a product.

Since Yang-Ming had been upgraded from a college to a university, we needed to restructure its organization, redraw many regulations and reallocate budget and resources. Most of these issues had to be discussed at various meetings with representatives of teachers and students.

Chang and I soon found that any general assembly on campus could be delayed beyond control, simply because of some participants' lengthy arguments.

At that time, Taiwan was undergoing political transformation. Ten-Whe Lee, who succeeded Chiang the junior as president of the Republic of China in Taiwan, radically restructured the legislature. The National Assembly, filled with elderly members, was dismantled. A new parliament was organized, national constitution ratified and the president elected by direct election.

Inspired by tremendous changes in politics, people loudly made comments about every issue; their opinions had been suppressed for too long. The whole society was full of noise. Hectic debates among lawmakers, sometimes accompanied by mass fights, were broadcast daily as 'soap' drama on television. In the meeting room of the university, professors did not behave violently but were sharp in their criticism.

Unlike most medical professors who knew little outside their profession, Chang understood the need to change a university from an 'ivory tower' to a community knowledge powerhouse. He planned to introduce academic-industrial cooperation into the campus, enrol more students to the relatively small-sized medical school and improve undergraduate teaching by introducing problem-based learning. His proposals were strongly resisted by some old-fashioned professors, who considered any change an increase in their workload. The democratic process in the university became a way to protect self-interest and the status quo.

After serving as president of the university for three years, Chang announced in 1999 he would not continue for a second term. Ovid J. L. Tzeng, a psychologist recruited by Chang to take the newly created position of vice-president, succeeded Chang's presidency. Tzeng was the first non-MD to serve as chief executive at Yang-Ming.

Yan-Hwa Wu, a female professor of biochemistry, succeeded me as the academic Dean. One year later, Tzeng was appointed as Minister of Education while Wu became the first female president in Yang-Ming. In fact, she was the first female president in any medical university in Taiwan.

Yang-Ming was progressing very well, thanks to strong governmental support and the simultaneous growth of its major teaching hospital, Taipei Veterans General Hospital. Many of Chang's policies were implemented after a new generation of young faculty members joined Yang-Ming.

Stepping down from the Deanship, I took a leave of absence from Yang-Ming to work at a drug company. When the leave of absence was completed two years later, I resigned from both the university and the hospital. I deeply appreciated the years I spent at Yang-Ming and Taipei Veterans General Hospital. It was the most productive period for my research. It was also the time Fumi and I brought up our daughters. I applied the most up-to-date theories in education to their upbringing.

As an academic Dean, I had several opportunities to attend educational conferences and learn from professional educators. I was raised under Taiwan's authoritative government and during my school years I obeyed the teachers, following their guides and never questioning my superiors. In London and Boston I was exposed to a free society but I did not fully realize traditional education in Taiwan was out of date until I served my Deanship.

Above all, I realized that the teacher should respect students. A student was an independent individual with his own values and judgments. The function of a teacher was not to feed knowledge to students and cast them in a mould he wanted them to fit into. Confucius, the master teacher in China born in 551 BC, pointed out that a teacher should teach students based on their talents. The best teacher identified the talents of students and helped them to develop their own future.

Confucius also emphasized that a good teacher should teach everyone, irrespective of their background. As long as the teacher was willing to spend time and effort discovering students' talents, he could tailor-make an education program for each of them. A teacher who only taught a group of highly selected, bright students was hardly the most respected one. Those who could teach the difficult ones were the real masters.

A direct beneficiary of such a concept was my elder daughter Ann. After she finished her senior high school in Taipei, I sent her to Los Angeles, California, for undergraduate education at Claremont, a beautiful town in the city's eastern suburbs.

Claremont Colleges were five colleges that shared a campus and common facilities. They operated like a federation of colleges. Each one maintained its own specialty and character. Several constituent members of Claremont Colleges, such as Pomona and Mckenna, were ranked among the top liberal arts colleges in the USA. The reputation of these colleges was not based on their research-oriented graduate schools, with the exception of an MBA program named after Peter Drucker, who had been teaching there since 1971. Drucker was respected by his followers as the man who invented management; his 39 books strongly influenced modern organization and management.

Pitzer College was one of the Claremont colleges. It was social science-oriented and emphasized individualized education, tailored to the career needs of each student. Ann, a foreign student unfamiliar with the environment of an American university, was kindly cared for by some of the faculty members at Pitzer. She lived in a dormitory on campus. At weekends, her uncle and aunt in the nearby town of Upland took her to stay in their house.

I advised Ann to study as wide a range as possible of academic disciplines during her first year. She could delay her choice of a major until she discovered her interest and talent. She graduated smoothly with a degree in biotechnology and management.

Ann returned to Taiwan and worked in Taipei and Hong Kong for two years. One day she told me that she would like to go to the United States again to study law. I immediately approved her proposal and promised to support her. My father and I were considering a career in law before we were pushed by our fathers to study medicine. This time, I was happy to know that she would like to complete the unfilled wishes of her father and grandfather.

She prepared all admission requirements for law school. She chose Tulane University in New Orleans for her law degree. I visited her once in Tulane. It was there I first met a handsome young man, Henry Shou-Hen Hung, my future son-in-law. He came from Taipei to study for a Master of Business Administration in New Orleans. They accompanied me on a tour of the city's French Quarter and we enjoyed spicy Cajun dishes.

Ann graduated from Tulane as a JD in June 2005. She was fortunate to leave New Orleans two months before hurricane Katrina flooded the city in August.

Next year, Ann successfully passed the bar examination in the State of New York and became a lawyer. She returned to Taipei and got married to Henry. At their wedding ceremony I gave them three pieces of advice. First, love rather than righteousness should prevail in a family; second, Henry should learn to be a good husband from his father and Ann a good wife from her mother; third, when someday they wondered why their partner had changed, they should know it was as a result of living together, not simply a fault in one side. I also shared a poem with the guests at the wedding banquet. I wrote it and sent it to Ann from London when she was a little girl waiting for me in Taipei; I only wished that she would be happy and healthy. I asked for nothing more from her.

Henry joined Fitch Ratings, a leading international credit rating agency. Ann accompanied Henry to work first in Singapore, then Shanghai, where Henry opened a branch office for Fitch.

As an academic physician on a fixed salary, financial conditions in my household were reasonably adequate but when my children wanted to study abroad, money was tight. Fumi founded Maxigen Enterprises, Inc. in 1988 to sell domestically made diagnostic kits. During many stages of my career, her supplementary income supported me so I could take a lower-paid but more meaningful job.

A Taiwanese company, General Biological Corporation, was founded to produce diagnostic kits for hepatitis. Originally, it was part of a national effort to eradicate hepatitis B infection among Taiwanese. Following the discovery of hepatitis C in 1989, this company commissioned a group of Taiwanese scientists to formulate the technology to produce a diagnostic kit for detecting hepatitis C infection. Facing strong competition from imported kits, the general manager of the company invited Fumi to take part in selling this new product. Fumi's medical background and previous experience at Proctor and Gamble helped her to boost sales. Imported kits led to sharp price cuts but the domestic brand was still able to dominate the market until a second-generation kit was developed.

When I was working at Yang-Ming and Taipei Veterans General Hospital, I was sitting on a Drug Evaluation Committee that gave advice to the Drug Bureau of the Ministry of Health regarding drug approval in Taiwan. In order to avoid a conflict of interest, I persuaded Fumi not to get involved in the business of pharmaceutical products. She founded Taiwan Biomedical Ltd. after I left the committee. That company invested in newly established biotechnology and drug companies. She and her company also helped to import artemisinin from China to Taiwan.

Artemisinin, the anti-malaria drug isolated from a Chinese medicinal herb, was produced only by a pharmaceutical company in China. Malaria had long been eradicated in Taiwan, but sporadic cases arrived from abroad. These patients developed serious symptoms after they came to Taiwan.

Many of them did not react to conventional anti-malaria treatments. Artemisinin was the drug of choice for them, the only drug that could save their lives. Experts in infectious diseases strongly urged Taiwanese health authorities to stock artemisinin and distribute it to the hospitals in case of emergency.

According to Taiwanese regulations, all imported drugs had to be produced by pharmaceutical factories recognized by the Drug Bureau in Taiwan. Many people had moved between Taiwan and mainland China during the 1990s; however, a system for Taiwanese government to recognize officially a Chinese drug factory had yet to be established.

Taiwanese Centres for Disease Control openly asked any company to import this product under a special license. Since it was a small and complicated business with little profit, only Fumi's company bid for the tender. I encouraged her to do so because I knew the importance of artemisinin during my tenure as a director of traditional medicine at Yang-Ming. By taking on this business, Fumi's company owned the first license to import a drug from China to Taiwan, even though this drug was supplied only to the Centres for Disease Control and not for sale to the general public.

A few years later, Fumi and some Taiwanese businesswomen were received by Ze-Min Jiang, then the Chairman of the People's Republic of China, in his office in Beijing. She was introduced to Jiang as the owner of a company that imported the first Chinese-made drug to Taiwan. Chiang was very happy to talk with them; the duration of the meeting was extended from half an hour to more than one hour. They chatted about subjects ranging from his early career as an engineer in a Shanghai factory to his favorite Alexandre Dumas novel, *La Dame aux Camelias*.

CHAPTER 22

The Pharmaceutical Industry in Taiwan. Clinical Drug Trials.

Taking a leave of absence from Yang-Ming University, I had my first experience in business at Genelabs in 1999. This action was not financially motivated; my income from the new job was not that different from my original salary. But in the middle of my career, I had an urge to try something new and significant.

Genelabs Biotechnology, Inc. was a company jointly invested by Genelabs Technologies, USA, the Taiwanese government's Development Fund and private investors such as Nina Wang in Hong Kong.

In order to transfer key technologies to Taiwan, the government set up a Development Fund to invest in early-stage high-tech companies that might require long-term funding. This fund played an important role in supporting the establishment of the computer and information industries in Taiwan.

Genelabs Technologies was a biotechnology company established by Frank Kong in the 1980s at Redwood City in the Bay area of northern California, USA. Kong, a Taiwanese-American, was a scientist and entrepreneur. An early project for this research-based company was the development of a diagnostic kit to detect the rare Hepatitis E. A few years later, Kong left the company to become a full-time investor. Irene Chow took the chairmanship, acted as CEO and shifted the focus of the company to drug development.

Chow was a charming lady; her undergraduate major in Taiwan was foreign languages, while in the USA she studied statistics in the graduate school. She worked at Ciba-Geigy, where she became a senior vice-president for drug development prior to the merger of the company with Sandoz to become Novartis. She had extensive experience in clinical drug trials, which required a sound knowledge in statistics.

The Taiwanese considered know-how in conducting clinical trials to be a key factor, urgently needed for the development of the biomedical and pharmaceutical industries.

Clinical trials of drugs could be classified into four phases.

In a phase one trial, a new drug that had never been used on humans was given to a small number of healthy volunteers. The initial dose was very low, then escalated gradually. The purpose of this phase was to test the safety of the drug. Some drugs with predicted toxicity, such as anti-cancer drugs, could be tested on volunteer patients.

In a phase two trial, the drug was given to a small number of patients to see whether the drug showed the effects observed in animal experiments.

In a phase three trial, a large number of patients was divided into two groups, one of them given the drug on trial, the other either a placebo or a commonly used drug for comparison. Patients were assigned to each group randomly. A professional term to describe the character of such a study was 'randomized controlled trial'. A phase three trial was mostly performed in several hospitals at the same time.

Once all three phases were completed, data collected in these trials would be submitted to the drug regulating authority, such as the Food and Drug Administration (FDA) in the USA for approval. If approved, this drug could be marketed and used widely on patients.

Phase four trials, also known as post-marketing trials, were follow-up studies after drugs were approved. Some of them were promotional activities by drug companies; doctors who had little experience of the new drug were encouraged to test the drug on a limited number of their patients.

Drug trials were complicated and expensive. When people talked about research and development of a new drug, research meant the discovery of the drug while the largest part of development was the clinical trials.

Before Genelabs introduced clinical trials that fulfilled FDA requirements, most clinical trials in Taiwan were phase four trials sponsored by multinational drug companies. The tested drugs had already been approved and used in Europe or America. The Drug Bureau in Taiwan approved a drug mainly based on data collected from clinical trials in the USA, UK, Japan, or Germany, not from trials in Taiwan.

While Taiwan was one of the world leaders in making high-tech products such as computers and semi-conductors, the pharmaceutical industry in Taiwan was poorly developed. Most Taiwanese drug companies were making off-patent drugs for domestic use. Taiwanese-made drugs could hardly be registered abroad; the inability to carry out clinical trials to international standards limited the ability of Taiwanese drug companies to promote their products to the international market. Government departments responsible for economic growth, as well as the medical community in Taiwan, wanted rapid improvement of clinical trials in Taiwan. It was not only vital to pharmaceutical industry, but also important for the future development of diagnostic kits and medical instruments. If Taiwanese doctors knew how to conduct effective clinical trials, the overall standard of medicine could be lifted.

Chow was the chairman of both Genelabs in the USA and Taiwan; she flew frequently across the Pacific to oversee the operation of the two companies. She hired Jen Chen, a chemist who worked with her at Ciba-Geigy, to be the general manager of Genelabs Biotechnology in Taiwan. I sat as Deputy Chairman on the board of Genelabs, Taiwan; I also acted as Chief Medical Officer to supervise the clinical trials and drug development projects within the company.

Most professors in Taiwanese medical colleges spent their leave-of-absence years working in another medical college or hospital. I was one of the few to work in business. What I did was encouraged because the government started to acknowledge the importance of academic-industrial cooperation. When I was working at Genelabs, the number of medical doctors serving in Taiwanese drug companies could be counted with fingers.

There was a clinical trial division in the Taipei office of Genelabs. The majority of staff were clinical research coordinators who went to hospitals to conduct clinical trials under the auspices of the principal investigator. Most of them had previous experience as nurses. We also employed clinical research associates to monitor the progress of trials, and statisticians to analyze the collected data.

The most important project we were executing was a phase three trial to see if DHEA was beneficial for the treatment of lupus erythematosus. Lupus was an immunological disease commonly seen in women of a young age. Incidence of this chronic and debilitating disease was higher among Chinese. Immune-suppressive drugs such as steroids were the standard treatment for it. Side effects of steroids were common and sometimes serious.

An American professor found DHEA effective for lupus in his laboratory. He persuaded Genelabs in the USA to start a multi-centre clinical trial in America. Genelabs Taiwan coordinated several hospitals in Taiwan to participate in this trial. All protocols and procedures of the trial in the USA were followed in Taiwan. By doing so, know-how in executing a clinical trial to an international standard could be completely transferred to Taiwan.

DHEA is naturally present in the human body. It is synthesized in the adrenal gland before being transformed into more potent steroids in other parts of the body. It was considered as a less potent, but safer alternative to the synthetic steroids commonly used for the treatment of immunological disorders. Since it was a known compound and sold as a healthy food in stores, Genelabs needed only a use patent to develop it into a prescription drug.

Patients enrolled into this trial were asked to maintain a minimal dose of steroids and took DHEA or a placebo tablet by random assignment. The frequency and severity of flare-ups in their symptoms were used as endpoints to evaluate the effect of DHEA.

In addition to DHEA for lupus, Genelabs Taiwan developed a new formulation for an anti-cancer drug, paclitaxel. This formulation reduced a specific chemical component when preparing paclitaxel injection solutions. That component was considered to induce many neurological side-effects in patients receiving the drug. Paclitaxel was isolated from the bark of the Pacific yew. Many other widely used anti-cancer drugs were also derived from natural sources.

Genelabs helped other drug companies to manage their clinical trials, acting as a contract research organization, commonly known as a CRO. By doing so, the clinical trial division could generate income to supplement its expenses.

During the two years I worked at Genelabs, we carried out around 30 clinical trials. Half of them were either initiated or completed when I was there. The initial and final stages of a clinical trial were the most important, because they involved protocol design or report-writing. These clinical trials covered different medical specialties including vaccines for children, contraceptives for women and drugs for asthma, peptic ulcers, diarrhea, hypertension, cancer, allergic rhinitis and psychological diseases. My knowledge of drug treatment was updated; I enjoyed this experience even though most of these trials were phase four with little academic value.

There were several Standard Operative Procedures, or SOP in short, for the management of clinical trials. Many documents had to be filled in, double-checked and filed. The purpose of these SOPs was to guarantee the quality of the trial. I found this very educational.

Genelabs Taiwan had a manufacturing plant that produced generic drugs and a research facility to develop new formulations in Hsinchu, 70km south of Taipei. There were many high-tech companies supported by excellent universities in the science park at Hsinchu. I regularly attended meetings there to supervise research and development projects. The decision to choose a new product for launching was challenging; several factors including technical feasibility, market size and the capability of the sales team all had to be considered. It was good brain exercise for me to participate.

By the time I left Genelabs, clinical trials for DHEA had not been completed. Later, after data from American and Taiwanese trials were combined and analyzed, this drug was found to be of little help in the treatment of lupus. It was safe with few side effects; it also improved osteoporosis in patients taking steroids to a small but significant extent. This was a reasonable finding because DHEA could be converted to an androgenic hormone that protected patients from osteoporosis. Disappointed with its overall effect, Genelabs dropped the project. In 2009, Genelabs in the USA was acquired by SmithKline Beecham Corporation. Genelabs in Taiwan was separated from Genelabs, USA; its name was changed to Genovate Biotechnology.

In addition to Genelabs, I was a board member of several organizations supporting the development of the pharmaceutical and biomedical industries in Taiwan, such as the Development Centre of Biotechnology and the Centre for Drug Evaluation. The quality of clinical trials improved in Taiwan year on year. Several new drugs were discovered by Taiwanese scientists; their early-phase clinical trials were carried out locally. Medical doctors participated in clinical trials not only for drug companies, but also for scientific investigations into unsolved clinical questions. Ethics committees, which protected patient rights during clinical trials, were organized in most medical centres.

The opening of the mainland Chinese market to Taiwanese pharmaceutical products improved the sales and profits of many Taiwanese drug companies. More and more pharmaceutical and medical instrument companies were listed on the stock market. The prospects for biomedical industry became much brighter. As one of the Taiwanese medical doctors who actively participated in accelerating these progresses, I was glad and proud to see all these changes.

A seventh-degree earthquake shook Taiwan on 21 September 1999. I was awakened in bed at night. Central Taiwan was most heavily damaged. More than 2,000 people died because of this natural disaster. We watched on television how people in foreign countries suffered from tsunamis and earthquakes, but the 21 September earthquake was personally experienced by many Taiwanese.

There was an earthquake in politics, too.

The Democratic Progress Party, commonly called the DPP, had been the strongest opposition against the ruling Nationalist Party for years. Several DPP leaders were either participants of the 1979 Kaohsiung demonstration for human rights or their defense lawyers in court.

Many local counties, including the capital city, Taipei, were controlled by the DPP. The mayor of Taipei, Sui-Pen Chen, was a rising political star. He was one of the human-rights lawyers. Vocal and energetic, the DPP chose him as a presidential candidate in 2000.

It was rumored that President Lee privately supported Chen, even though Lee was the leader of the Nationalist Party. Lee was sympathetic to the DPP policy favoring an independent Taiwan.

Chen won the election. Fifty-six years' rule by the Nationalist Party in Taiwan, since the Japanese left at the end of the Second World War, was over. Lee was expelled from the Nationalist Party one year later by his former comrades. Chen sent a signal of peace to China during his inaugural speech guaranteeing that he would not declare Taiwanese independence or take a hostile position towards mainland China.

Chen was re-elected in 2004. A mysterious shot was fired at him and made a small wound on his abdomen while he was campaigning one day before the election. A large number of voters offered him last-minute sympathy in the ballot. A deceased suspect was blamed for this assassination attempt, but the nature of this plot was never fully disclosed.

Shortly after he completed his second term and stepped down, Chen and his family members were found to have accepted large bribes from businessmen and illegally transferred them to accounts abroad. He personally admitted it in public. Indicted and sentenced to 20 years in prison, his plea for release on medical reasons was rejected.

The DPP lost the presidential elections to In-Chow Ma of the Nationalist Party in 2008 and 2012. Ma was a lawyer with a doctoral degree from Harvard. He served as a secretary to former president Chiang the junior. Handsome and athletic, he was popular among female voters. He kept himself away from businessmen, as had Chiang the junior. Being a son of mainlander parents and born in Hong Kong, his policies to establish closer economic and political ties with China were repeatedly boycotted by DPP members of parliament.

Hong Kong was returned from the UK to China in 1997. I watched the handover ceremony on television. To me and many others, it was a testimony of history. When my leave-of-absence from Yang-Ming and my service at Genelabs were completed in 2001, I did not return to Yang-Ming. I resigned from all my jobs in Taiwan, including a professorship at Yang-Ming and my clinical appointment at Taipei Veterans General Hospital. I decided to move to Hong Kong and start a new career in China. I was just over 50 and willing to take the risk to give myself a totally different lifestyle.

CHAPTER 23

Biotechnology Companies in China. H&Q Asia Pacific and Sinogen.

M y shift from academic physician to businessman surprised many who knew me. That I gave up all my titles and positions in Taiwan to work in China was beyond their imagination. There had never been a Taiwanese medical doctor who dared to do so, not to mention a professor of medicine.

I was hired by H&Q Asia Pacific to act as chief executive officer of Sinogen, Inc.

H&Q, a boutique investment bank based in San Francisco, California, was founded by William Hambrecht and George Quist in 1968. It was the underwriter for the initial public offering of high-tech companies such as Apple Computer, Genentech and Adobe Systems. In 1999, it was acquired by Chase Manhattan Bank.

In 1986, Ta-Lin Hsu founded H&Q Asia Pacific as a branch of H&Q. It was the oldest and most established private equity firm in Asia Pacific, managing capital of more than US$2bn in its funds.

Hsu studied physics at Taiwan University, then he studied electrical engineering and got a PhD from the University of California at Berkley. He worked at IBM before joining H&Q. He was invited by the Taiwanese government to open the first office for H&Q Asia Pacific in Taipei. He introduced the concept of venture capital to Taiwan and helped many Taiwanese technology companies, such as Acer Computer, to raise funds and grow into internationally well-known giants.

H&Q Asia Pacific is now an independent company with offices in the financial centres of major Asia-Pacific countries, including Shanghai, Tokyo, Hong Kong, Seoul and Singapore.

Tsu-Der Lee, my dentist friend who served with me as a resident at Taipei Medical College Hospital in the 1970s, joined H&Q Asia Pacific in the 1990s. When Hsu opened a new office in China, he appointed Lee as the general manager. Starbucks in Beijing was one of their widely publicized investments.

Lee recommended me to Hsu. In previous years, Lee had sometimes asked me for advice on proposals submitted to the Taipei office of H&Q. I guessed Hsu knew that I was a cautious man who always gave critical comments instead of making risky suggestions.

I hesitated before accepting this job. What worried me most was whether I could return to Taiwan and resume my career as an academic physician. Following the referee system, which was commonly used when a journal accepted or rejected a paper, I listed three senior professors who I considered wise and respectable. I would consult them; if two of them chose either yes or no, I would follow their advice.

Benjamin Chiang told me if he were younger, he would take this job. I was surprised to hear such a straightforward suggestion from the most powerful and respected physician in Taiwan.

Luke S. Chang, former president of Yang-Ming University, also advised me to take the new job. There was no need for me to ask a third wise man. I accepted the offer, signed a three-year contract with H&Q Asia Pacific and submitted my resignation to Yang-Ming and Taipei Veterans General Hospital. I could no longer apply for a leave of absence since its maximum length was two years; I had already spent two years at Genelabs.

Biotech was a small but important part of Hsu's investment in China. He set up the fully owned Sinogen, Inc. in Hong Kong. With Wei-Ming Group of Beijing University as a partner, Sinogen owned majority shares in two biotech companies in China. Shenzhen Kexing produced interferon for the treatment of hepatitis B while Shandong Kexing produced erythropoietin for anemia and G-CSF for leucopenia, which was a lack of white blood cells in the body. Interferon was produced by cultured bacteria, while erythropoietin and G-CSF were produced by cultured kidney cells.

All these drugs were biotechnology products first made by American companies such as Genentech and Amgen. Their patents had expired so Kexing could legally produce them in China. Such generic versions of biological drugs were called biosimilars; there was no approval pathway for biosimilars in USA, although several of them had been approved in Europe.

Wei-Ming Group was one of the business groups owned by Beijing University. Wei-Ming, or 'not named', was the name of a lake on the university campus. Wei-Ming Group's businesses focused on biomedical products, while other groups such as Fan-Zeng focused on information technology and real estate etc. All senior staff in these groups were faculty members of the university.

The general manager for both Wei-Ming Group and Shenzhen Kexing was Ai-Hwa Pan, a medical doctor who became a research scientist and entrepreneur. He was interesting, capable and creative. Since he was in charge of two companies, a conflict of interest between the two business entities was sometimes inevitable. He later chose to serve full-time at Wei-Ming in Beijing; his position at Shenzhen Kexing was succeeded by a female accountant from Beijing University.

Sinogen shared an office with other H&Q Asia Pacific staff in Hong Kong at the Pacific Place of Admiralty; one of the most significant business addresses on the island. Every week, I took either the bus or the ferry to Shenzhen and stayed there for a few days.

Shenzhen was a Chinese city at the border with Hong Kong. It was developed from a small village into a modern metropolitan city after China adopted an open policy in the late 1970s. Unlike Hong Kong or nearby Chinese cities, most citizens in Shenzhen came from other provinces in China, so the language commonly used there was Mandarin Chinese, not Cantonese which was popular in Hong Kong. It was convenient for me because I knew little Cantonese. At the time I was working there, Shenzhen was a special zone in China; ordinary Chinese were required to get permission to enter it.

Guangzhou, capital of Guangdong province and the largest city in southern China, was 150km west of Shenzhen. It was known as Canton to many Europeans. Guangzhou, Shenzhen, Hong Kong and Macau were major cities in the Pearl River Delta where more than 100 million people were living.

Shenzhen Kexing was one of the earliest biotech companies in China. Its interferon dominated the Chinese market. Interferon was the only therapy for hepatitis B before other anti-viral agents became available. There were 300 employees in Shenzhen Kexing, and 22 sales offices in major cities all over China. Most of its senior staffs were graduates from top universities in China.

Operations for Shandong Kexing were much smaller. Shandong was a province in northern China. It was the birthplace of Confucius.

Once every two to three weeks, I flew back to Taipei to have a break at home. Since I travelled frequently, I stayed in hotels instead of renting an apartment when I was in Hong Kong or Shenzhen.

Two months after I joined Sinogen in 2001, the World Trade Centre in New York and the Pentagon in Washington DC were attacked by hijackers. On that day, I attended a meeting with Hsu, Lee and other H&Q staff at the Grand Hyatt in Shanghai, and then took the last flight of the day returning to Hong Kong. In the airport, I noticed heavily armed soldiers patrolling. That was unusual, but I did not pay much attention to it. Switching on the television, I saw the terrible pictures of the two burning towers after the two suicide jets hit the skyscrapers.

Everyone was shocked; the whole world was in chaos. Security at airports was so tight that air travel nearly came to a halt. However, I had to fly to the United States. Sinogen had business there.

Sinogen was actively soliciting partners and investors from America. We were in the process of negotiating with some American drug companies for co-operative projects. Besides, Sinogen owned a small research company called EGen Corporation in San Diego in southern California, and the headquarters of H&Q Asia Pacific was located at Palo Alto near San Francisco. I had to go to America to attend several business meetings on behalf of Sinogen.

In the aftermath of the 9/11 attacks, I flew several times to America, including a trip to Miami, Florida. The cabin of the flight was nearly empty; my luggage and my body were thoroughly inspected at every airport where I transited.

In China, I attended all the executive meetings on sales, production, research and development at Shenzhen Kexing. Sometimes, I drank at dinner parties with staff there; they were extremely good at drinking Chinese spirits, which I tried to avoid.

In early 2003, many patients in nearby Chinese cities around Shenzhen were diagnosed to have a severe flu. Birds were suspected of spreading the flu, so we were advised not to eat chicken. Besides, burning vinegar was supposed to disinfect the air and prevent the flu, so vinegar was out of stock in every shop. However, the health authorities and media in China did not provide any information about this disease.

In March, the Dean of the Medical College at the Chinese University of Hong Kong claimed in a press conference that many of his students and staff were infected with an unusual type of flu. In tears, he asked the Hong Kong government to take action to isolate patients and seal off the hospital in order to prevent the spread of the infection. Before his public announcement, Hong Kong government was trying to cover up the severity of this epidemic. Tracing back, a Chinese medical doctor from Guangzhou who sought medical treatment in Hong Kong spread the disease during his stay in a Hong Kong hotel. The Secretary for Health, Welfare and Food in Hong Kong was forced to resign owing to his poor handling of the outbreak.

This disease was named Severe Acute Respiratory Syndrome, or SARS in short. Its causative virus was identified later.

In early April, I went to Beijing to attend a meeting with Wei-Ming Group. After the meeting, I planned to spend the weekend there on vacation. At that time, not a single media outlet in China had reported the news of SARS. Our Chinese colleagues who were well connected with local hospitals warned us to leave Beijing as soon as possible, because all major hospitals were packed with SARS patients and many of them died. I took the earliest flight back to Hong Kong, where preventive measures had been taken. It was later reported that a businessman who sold vinegar in Guangzhou caught this disease and carried it to northern China.

A 72-year-old medical doctor, Yan-Yong Jiang, wrote a letter to the media to disclose the actual SARS situation in Beijing. He disobeyed the order from his superiors to remain silent in public. As a result of his action, the mayor of Beijing and the Minister of Health in China were dismissed for the cover-up of the crisis, and the Chinese government launched a massive public health campaign to contain the spread of the infection.

It was a dreadful disease; thousands were infected and hundreds died, many of them were hospital staff such as medical doctors and nurses. Those who survived the infection suffered from severe lung damage.

When SARS was spreading in Hong Kong, Hong Kong residents were asked to be quarantined for two weeks if they entered Taiwan. Lee phoned me from Taipei, asking me if I would fly back to Taiwan as soon as possible. I told him that I was the only one from H&Q Asia Pacific to take care of the business of Sinogen in Hong Kong and China; I could not leave at that critical moment. I chose to stay.

It was interesting that few cases of SARS were reported in Shenzhen, except some patients who developed symptoms soon after they came to Shenzhen from other cities. Shenzhen was located between Hong Kong and Guangzhou where SARS was spreading like wildfire. It was most likely that fresh air in this newly built modern city played an important role, since Hong Kong and Guangzhou were much more crowded. Fresh air was considered by some SARS experts as an effective means of preventing SARS spreading.

Shenzhen Kexing was operating as usual. There was a sudden increase in the demand for interferon. No study had been done to prove the therapeutic effect of interferon in SARS; but it was used by many medical staff to prevent themselves from being infected. The only reason for them to do so was that interferon was an anti-viral agent.

In an emergency meeting at Shenzhen Kexing, I discussed with company executives how to manage this condition. Should we promote the sale of interferon for the treatment of SARS? Should we raise the price or stockpile our goods until we could sell them at a higher price? Should we expand our production line? Should we sell interferon directly to customers instead of selling it through our local agents?

Almost instantaneously, I persuaded everyone to do what we should do as a responsible and honest company.

We should not promote interferon as a treatment for SARS, because there was no scientific evidence to support it. In fact, there was no need to do so because the demand was very strong already. Companies that advertised such an application were punished by the government after SARS was over; Kexing was not one of them.

We should not raise the price either. It was not only unethical but also illegal. Local government offices had records for the price of our products; it was illegal to change without prior permission from them. Companies who inflated the price were fined later, Kexing was not.

We could not predict how long the epidemic would last. It took months before we could purchase the equipment to expand our production line. Eventually, SARS was over in early summer when the temperature was raised. Some companies who invested in expanding their capacity lost a large amount of cash, Kexing did not.

Finally, direct selling to customers was a breach of our contract with local sales agents. It would damage our future co-operation. However, I suggested that Kexing would ship interferon to a local agent only when money owed to Kexing was paid in full. The management team had long been worried about the large sums of accounts receivable. Kexing did not make a fortune from SARS, but its financial figures improved after it.

During the SARS period, few people walked in the streets; if they did, they all wore a mask. The restaurants and shops were nearly empty. There were no tourists; all meetings were cancelled. I did not return to Taipei for three months, therefore I did not take care of SARS patients in Taiwan, where SARS started in April. However, I was probably the only Taiwanese medical doctor who personally observed the spread of SARS in China and Hong Kong.

Shenzhen Kexing had the technology to produce human insulin using recombinant DNA technology. Diabetes was becoming very common in China but insulin was produced there by the traditional method of slaughtering pigs. Unlike interferon, which was effective at very low doses, insulin had to be produced in large quantities to meet demand. Shenzhen Kexing planned to build a new, state-of-the-art plant to produce recombinant human insulin. I made a large effort to find investors and partners, and to supervise the design of the new plant. Unfortunately, this project did not materialize. Shares in Shenzhen Kexing owned by H&Q Asia Pacific were sold to a local Chinese company several years after I left Sinogen.

At the end of three years in Hong Kong and China, I was offered a job that I could hardly resist: vice-president of my alma mater medical college. By then it had been promoted to Taipei Medical University.

CHAPTER 24

Last View of Ancestors' Shrine.
Eight Hundred Years of Family History.

Being the only Taiwanese in Sinogen and its subsidiaries in China, most Chinese colleagues were curious about me and always helpful to me. I established a friendship with many of them.

Zang-Liang Chen was a vice-president of Beijing University; he was also chairman of Wei-Ming Group. After obtaining a PhD from the University of Washington in Seattle, Washington, he returned to China and led research into cloning a piece of DNA from the fossilized egg of a dinosaur. They reported their findings in the prestigious journal *Science*. The source of that DNA fragment was however considered as contamination by other scientists who did not believed DNA could be preserved for 1,000 centuries. An extremely smart young molecular biologist and administrator, he was later appointed as president of the China Agricultural University.

Kuang-Yang Shen was the general manager of Shandong Kexing. Once he told me that he was born and educated in Quanzhou in Fukien Province. That was the place where my great-grandfather was born.

My grandfather left behind the address of our family house in Quanzhou. It was an address from the Qing dynasty in the late 19th century. During the unrest years soon after the Japanese took over Taiwan, he and his brother made a short visit to that address.

The two big Chinese characters, Xinku, which meant 'new warehouse', were inscribed on the tombstone of my ancestors who died in Taiwan. I had been told since my childhood that Xinku was the place of our ancestors' house in Quanzhou.

During the half-century of rule by the Japanese and another half-century of hostility between the governments in Taiwan and mainland China, none of our family members in Taiwan were able to return to that address. I tried to find it on the map but in vain. There was no village called Xinku, the name of the village could have been changed during the past one hundred years.

I told Shen the story of how my family moved to Taiwan in the late 19th century, I also mentioned to him how I tried and failed to find the address. He kindly expressed his willingness to help. I gave him all the information, including names of my great-grandfather and his two sons who were born in Quanzhou.

A few months later, he told me that Hui-Huang Chen, who was a friend of his, had found my ancestors' house. I was very excited so I immediately arranged a trip there.

In November 2001, Fumi and I flew to Xiamen, where we hired a limousine to drive us to Quanzhou, 200km north of Xiamen.

Chen, a man of my age, met us in downtown Quanzhou. He had been at university with Shen. Driving to my ancestors' house, he gave us information regarding the house and its surroundings.

In fact, Xinku was not the name of a village; it was the name of the clan which my ancestors and I belonged to. The name of the village was Shuitou, or 'water head'. There was indeed the name Shuitou in the address left by my grandfather. Shuitou was a popular name, in many counties there could be a village named Shuitou. Shuitou, where my ancestors lived, was part of Shishi City.

Quanzhou was later divided into several regions; many of them such as Shishi were developed during subsequent decades. No wonder it was difficult for me to locate the address of my ancestors' house.

As we were approaching our destiny, I fell into silence. Retrospectively, I would say it was the most sacred journey of my life. Like a pilgrim, I went there not only for myself, but for my great-grandparents and their sons. Their spirits accompanied me.

Chen parked his car outside the village. We walked through the narrow, stone-paved streets. Most houses were old and built with yellowish stones. We stopped in front of a wooden gate, a red lantern with a Chinese character of Hong hung outside the wall. A middle-aged lady opened the door; Chen explained to her that we were guests from Taiwan.

We entered a small court and saw an old man. He was the most senior member of this house. He shared with my father the same first character of the given name, so I immediately recognized that he ranked as my father's generation. He was my paternal uncle. In traditional Chinese families, all members of the same generation had the same first character in their two-character given names.

After greeting each other, he showed me a book of 400 pages; it was a family book hand-written with black brush pen in 1885. He turned to a page where the names of my great-grandfather, Bao-Xu, his wife and two sons were clearly written.

Chen found my ancestors' house mainly by using these names. I could imagine how much effort he had made for me. He must have checked many documents so he could bring me back to the exact site where my ancestors came from. A broken linkage between the generations in Taiwan and those in mainland China was connected. I could hardly say how much I thanked Chen. Without him, the last wish of my great-grandfather and grandfather that someday their offspring should go back to their ancestors' house would never come true.

I asked the elder man if there was a place called 'House of a Hundred Footsteps'. He asked a boy to take Fumi and me there. It was a huge complex of houses occupying a large area; in the centre was the ancestors' shrine. The roof of it had nearly collapsed; a few incense sticks were burning in a vase on a small table. I was surprised and felt sorry to see it.

Later I was told that all family members had shared the whole building complex as a commune, until a system allowing individual ownership of property started after economic reform. The one who got the part containing the shrine sold it to an outsider. This shrine, along with most houses surrounding it, would soon be pulled down. I was just in time to have a last look of it. I guessed it must be the place where my great-grandparents and their sons paid their last respects to their ancestors before leaving for Taiwan. It was also the place my grandfather visited during his stay there; otherwise he would not remember a House of a Hundred Footsteps and repeatedly describe it to his sons, including my father.

The elder man promised to give me a copy of the family book. A few months later, I flew there again and brought it back to Taipei. I made several photocopies of it and gave them to my cousins who were living in Taiwan, Japan and America.

From the family book, I traced my ancestors back to the Southern Song Dynasty of the 12th century. Names of every ancestor from the first generation of this clan to the 23rd generation of my great-grandfather were written on it. Most of them had their birth and death dates recorded. I understood from this book that I am the 26th generation of this Xinku clan of Hong.

During the culture revolution, members of our family tried hard to hide the family book in secrecy, otherwise it would be burned by Red guards. Not many Chinese families kept their family books; this book was saved because Shuitou was a small fishing village which few Red guards visited.

Fumi and I were happy to know that most members of the Hong family married those of the Wang family in the village. Hong and Wang were two big families there. Fumi's family name was Wang, but her ancestors did not come from Shuitou. They came to Taiwan during the late Qing dynasty from another town in Quanzhou. Her family shared many common experiences with mine; her grandparents had businesses in mainland China, while her parents were educated under Japanese rule. I found that many of my best friends were the offspring of immigrants who came to Taiwan from Fukien during the late Qing dynasty.

Books on Chinese history provided more information for me. Ancestors of the Hong and Wang families moved from Henan Province in northern China to the south to escape the civil war of the Tang dynasty during the ninth century. A general of the Wang family established an independent state in Fukien. Ancestors of the Hong clan in Xinku were most likely a branch of immigrants from Henan; they moved from some other part of Fukien before settling down in Shuitou in the 12th century.

In addition to friends in China, I was privileged to know some renowned people in Hong Kong.

H&Q Asia Pacific invited several experts in biotechnology from Hong Kong to sit in the boards of Sinogen and Shenzhen Kexing. One of them was Shian-Dow Kung. A refugee from mainland China living in Hong Kong, he studied horticulture in Taiwan; then went to Canada for his PhD. He worked in several American universities before he was appointed as a vice-president at the newly opened Hong Kong University for Science and Technologies. More senior than me, he told me many of his experiences in Hong Kong and Northern America; he was very supportive of me during the years I served at Sinogen. In his seventies, he got a doctoral degree from the Department of Psychology at Beijing University.

Nina Wang was the richest woman in Asia. She was an investor in Genelabs, both in the USA and Taiwan. I had known her since I was working at Genelabs. In Hong Kong, I approached her to see if she was interested in investing in Sinogen.

Her husband was kidnapped twice; she paid the ransom for him but he did not return the second time. Her husband left her a fortune which grew to around US$20bn. It was said that she owned 200 buildings in Hong Kong and a joke rumored that she went shopping not for clothes but for real estate. She was thrifty and did not wear expensive suits or jewelry. She tied her hair into two small bunches, a style only seen on little girls in the Chinese countryside. In Taiwan, she was relaxed and ate at common, popular restaurants easily; while in Hong Kong, she paid great attention to her security. Her Cadillac was bullet-proof and her house was located on the top floor of her company. I was told to pass through many narrow corridors and thick doors to enter her guest room, which was simply decorated. She died in 2010 aged 70. It was said that she did not actively seek medical treatment for her ovarian cancer because she was engaged in a lawsuit with her father-in-law involving her right to the fortune inherited from her husband. She was an interesting lady, friendly but always asking sharp questions.

I travelled extensively in China. Sometimes I visited branch offices or attended meetings outside Shenzhen. Sometimes I travelled alone, or with Fumi only. Without companionship from my Chinese colleagues, I became a backpacker during my vacation. It was an extraordinary experience; I strolled around attractions that had been famous for thousands of years. They were described by many poets and writers in classic literary works. I visited more than two-thirds of the provinces in China during my years at Sinogen.

The mileage on Cathay Pacific Airlines I accumulated during these three years was enough for me to redeem a business class air ticket to fly around the world. Before starting my new job in Taipei, I took this opportunity to spend a few days each in London, Boston and Los Angeles, places that were milestones at various stages of my career.

CHAPTER 25

Taipei Medical University.
Reform of Medical Education.

os Angeles was the last stop on my flight around the world. There I attended a gathering of TMU alumni; many of them had been my friends when I was a medical student. The president and several senior professors at TMU came from Taipei to join us. As a newly appointed vice-president, I was warmly greeted by all participants.

Fumi picked me up at the airport when I returned to Taipei on an early morning in August 2004. The rising sun brightened the sky, clouds above the green hills were colorful, the weather was warm and the air fresh; I was full of confidence and happiness.

There were five colleges, 300 full-time teachers and 4,000 students in TMU. In addition to a university hospital in the campus, TMU operated Wan Fang Hospital as its second major teaching hospital. Wen-Ta Chiu, vice-president of clinical affairs, was the superintendent at Wan Fang Hospital.

I had been sitting on the board of directors at TMU for five years since I was academic Dean at Yang-Ming University. In order to take the job of vice-president, I had to resign from the board as required by university regulations. Hsien-Chen Hsieh, former chairman of the board, actively solicited me and other alumni to join the board. A medical graduate of Taiwan University and well-known parasitologist, Hsieh spent several years in Africa as a consultant to the World Health Organization. He had been Dean of Kaohsiung Medical College in southern Taiwan for nearly 20 years. After retirement from Kaohsiung, he became chairman of my alma mater medical college. He was a classmate of my father at high school. A devoted and selfless scholar, he was respected by many, including me, as one of the most distinguished medical educators in Taiwan.

Two years before I joined TMU, the board of directors under chairman Chen-Wen Wu invited Chung Y. Hsu, a professor of neurology at Washington University, St. Louis, to become the president of the university. Hsu had spent his entire medical career in the USA since he graduated from Taiwan University.

Wu was an expert in cancer research and administration. He founded a National Health Research Institute in Taiwan. He succeeded Hsieh to become the chairman of the board after Hsieh passed away.

Hsu was a few years older than me. Determined to transform TMU into a research-based medical university of an international caliber, he brought many new ideas to TMU and acted very fast to implement his grand plan. Not all staff and students were able to catch up with him. The board was in search of someone who had prior knowledge of TMU to work with him. I was chosen because I was an alumnus and a board member. Besides, my track record at Yang-Ming University and Taipei Veterans General Hospital was complementary to Hsu's experience in the USA.

Hsu first changed the system by which the university hired new faculty members. In most universities in Taiwan, including TMU, senior members of a department were decisive in choosing a new teacher for the department. Most of the time, they picked one of their former students. All faculty members in a department became a clone of teachers who hardly had any different ideas from the senior ones. In the worst scenario, they put their interest ahead of that of the students. Hsu organized a committee to oversee the hiring process, making sure it was open and fair to all applicants. He particularly asked the committee to review why a better-qualified applicant was rejected. I was assigned by him to take part in this committee.

He reformed the structure of faculty evaluation committees for promoting teachers to higher academic ranks. Preliminary decisions at departmental level were abolished; all candidates for promotion were reviewed first by the committee of their college, then by a university committee. A department head could not reject an application for promotion; he could only give his comments on the candidate to the committees. This change required a revision of university regulations. The revision had to be passed by the majority of faculties in the general assembly of the university before it was sent to the Ministry of Education for approval.

Hsu assigned me to lead the revision. After numerous meetings, the new regulations were passed and TMU became the first university in Taiwan to have such a system.

He considered most graduate programs too small in scale to function well. He proposed to merge many institutes. For example, all master's programs operated by basic medical institutes were merged to form a new Institute of Medical Sciences. Many directors of institutes would lose their titles and their right to allocate budgets. Resistance from them was strong; Hsu directed me to work with senior executives of the university to complete the restructuring.

He recruited new college Deans and department heads from outside; many of them had little previous relationship with TMU. This was unusual in Taiwan, where senior professors who had been serving on campus for years were traditionally appointed to such positions. What he did was common practice in American or European universities; he did not understand why it could not be followed in Taiwan. I was appointed by him to chair several recruitment committees; I supported him strongly in this issue and offended many senior professors, some of them were my teachers or friends when I was a student.

Hsu emphasized the importance of the application of computers in teaching and administration. Under him, TMU invested heavily in the infrastructure of information technologies. He assigned me to lead a team to construct brand new software to incorporate all finance-related functions including accounting, purchasing and logistics in the university. He also asked me to work with the personnel office to update all the data in its files.

I acted as the director of a Faculty Development Centre. New regulations to evaluate the performance of teachers in teaching and research were enforced. Students' feedback was actively solicited. Teachers and department heads were asked to respond to comments and suggestions from students. Courses for improving teaching skills were provided to teachers. I personally designed a Case Based Integrated Teaching, or C-BIT, to coordinate the pre-clinical and clinical teachings for medical students. More than 200 teachers volunteered to take part in preparing 30 teaching manuals for this project. When the Ministry of Education carried out a nationwide inspection of universities, I supervised every department and institute in TMU to prepare for the site-visit. By doing so, I had a very good understanding of the details of the campus. I organized a book club for faculties, and encouraged interaction between faculties among different departments and colleges. After all these efforts, the Ministry of Education voted TMU one of the best universities in teaching.

Working with a team of neuroscientists, Hsu wrote a research proposal on cerebrovascular disease to apply for a top-notch research grant in Taiwan. This proposal was approved by the Minister of Education. Under Hsu's leadership, research quality and productivity at TMU were improved substantially.

Having recently returned to Taiwan, Hsu spent a great amount of his time outside the campus networking. I signed most documents for day-to-day operations, leaving only those related to financial, personnel and legal issues to him for the final decision.

Hsu was an active supporter for the Democratic Progressive Party when he was in the United States. However, he strictly maintained his political neutrality on campus and never abused his authority in persuading any staff to take part in political activities. I respected him very much for this.

The only time I kept silent was regarding his proposal to replace cadaver dissection in anatomy class with web-based teaching. There was a cry against it among students and teachers. It was true that parts of anatomical knowledge could be better learned through a computer, which incorporated three-dimensional images such as CT and MRI scans of the body. It was also true that in some foreign medical schools, dissection was abolished from their curriculums. However, the symbolic significance of dissection to a medical student was difficult to replace with a computer. On an anatomy table, the student touched death for the first time; it was one of the most unforgettable moments in a medical career.

In spring every year, when many Chinese went to the tombs of their ancestors to pay their respect, there was a ceremony at TMU to pay tribute to those who had donated their bodies for dissection. They were called silent teachers. In the auditorium, faculty members, students and families of the deceased watched movies and slides showing the lives of these silent teachers as well as interviews with their families. It was always a moving moment for me and many others who attended this occasion.

Hsu had his weaknesses. He often delayed meetings and colleagues were asked to work overtime till very late. He changed his mind frequently and gave new orders different to the ones he gave before. His colleagues were confused. Sometimes I had to show the documents on which he had written his decision to remind him that he had already given his orders. I guessed these problems arose mainly because he treated his staff as his students or research fellows.

Hsu was a very good researcher; most members of his team in the United States were graduate students or fellows. They worked day and night to finish their training so they could leave the laboratory as early as possible to find a better job. In doing research, the supervisor gave his staff new ideals and encouraged them to change their minds from time to time. Such a working style could not be applied to full-time university staff with families and personal lives.

Hsu made an enormous contribution to TMU; he radically changed my alma mater from a family-style small university to a competitive, mission-oriented enterprise. He resigned three months before his second term was completed and moved to China Medical University in central Taiwan. I was appointed by the board as acting president until a new president was elected.

During these three months, I signed the diploma for the class of 2008, attended the commencement ceremony and delivered a speech which I carefully prepared. At a similar occasion 34 years previously, I gave a speech demonstrating our dissatisfaction on behalf of all students leaving the school. This time, I was the chief executive of the school; the title of my talk to medical students was 'Never give up hope'.

Tsu-Der Lee, a dental resident when the hospital on campus first opened its doors and a former general manager of H&Q Asia Pacific in Beijing, replaced Wu as the chairman of the board at TMU. The board of directors elected Wen-Ta Chiu, superintendent of Wan Fang Hospital as the new president of the university. I was appointed as the successor to Chiu at Wan Fang Hospital.

PART SIX

*Searching for the Value of
Medicine and Life*

CHAPTER 26

Wan Fang Hospital.
Improvements in Quality of Patient Care.

Without previous experience in hospital administration, I took the new challenge to lead Wan Fang Hospital in the summer of 2008.

This hospital was built by the Taipei city government; it did not open its doors for four years after the building was completed because the city council did not pass the operating budget. Most government hospitals, including all municipal hospitals in Taipei, were losing money while private hospitals provided good service and at the same time were making a profit. The city council requested that the city government find a non-governmental organization to operate this new hospital.

In the main campus of Taipei Medical College, there was a teaching hospital in which I served as a resident before I went to London. The college was looking for a new hospital to accommodate the large number of students for clinical training.

The city government and the college signed a contract. The college would purchase equipment, hire staff and take all financial responsibility for the hospital. A rent of around US$1m would be paid to the city government every year. Wan Fang Hospital would continue the public health functions of a municipal hospital, such as health education to local citizens and medical care for the poor. The contract could be renewed every nine years.

The college appointed a young neurosurgeon, Wen-Ta Chiu as the superintendent of the new hospital. Chiu was one of the three vice-superintendents of the hospital in the campus. The other two vice-superintendents, Chii-Ruey Tseng and Chih-Hsiung Wu later became Dean of the medical college and superintendent of the campus hospital respectively. Tseng was an expert in test-tube babies while Wu was a prominent surgeon. After Taipei Medical College became Taipei Medical University in 2000, they all made great contributions to the growth of the university and its teaching hospitals. Their superintendent at the campus hospital, An-Jun Chen, should be credited as a great mentor who knew how to find talented young men, train them and develop them.

Chen was a professor of obstetrics and gynecology with complete clinical training in Baltimore, Maryland at hospitals affiliated with Johns Hopkins. Well-trusted by patients, he delivered my daughters, Ann and Wan. After retirement, he suffered from blindness as a complication of diabetes and hypertension; he devoted so much time to work that he did not pay enough attention to his own health. He was a great doctor and teacher, sincerely thanked and remembered by many young doctors.

In 1997, Wan Fang Hospital was opened to the public. Chiu and his colleagues had to clean the building before instruments were moved in. They found many dogs, rats and snakes in the basement. Most likely these snakes came from a hill at the back of the hospital.

Chiu held a doctoral degree in public health in addition to his clinical training in neurosurgery. He was not an alumnus of Taipei Medical University but he had been working at the university for decades. A hard-working man with outstanding leadership skills, Chiu established his reputation as one of the best hospital administrators in Taiwan. The rapid growth of Wan Fang Hospital under his management in every aspect, including clinical service, teaching and research, astonished everyone. Chiu handed over the position of superintendent to me and succeeded Hsu as the president of Taipei Medical University.

Hospitals in Taiwan were classified into three types: medical centre, regional hospital and district hospital. Insurance reimbursement varied according to the type of hospital. Among 400 hospitals, only around 20 were medical centres, all historic in reputation and large in scale. Being a medical centre, a hospital had many privileges and responsibilities.

It was remarkable that Wan Fang passed the thorough inspection by an accreditation committee organized jointly by the Ministries of Health and Education to become a medical centre in 2005, eight years after its first opening. With 500 acute beds, 100 beds in a skilled nursing home, and around 200 beds for special purposes such as emergency, critical care, isolation, dialysis, and psychiatry, Wan Fang was the smallest medical centre in Taiwan.

Chiu's most important tool for improving the quality of Wan Fang was external evaluation. Wan Fang volunteered to be inspected by many domestic and international organizations and passed their accreditations. Among them was JCI, or Joint Commission International.

Most American hospitals that received insurance reimbursement, including Medicaid and Medicare, were accredited by the Joint Commission, a Chicago-based organization that evaluated and accredited more than 20,000 health care institutions in the United States.

JCI was a division of the Joint Commission. JCI provided accreditation to healthcare organizations outside the United States. More than 400 hospitals around the world volunteered to apply for a JCI accreditation and passed it.

JCI sent a team of surveyors to stay for a few days in the hospital for an on-site survey. The number of surveyors and the length of their stay varied according to the size of the hospital. For Wan Fang, JCI used to send four surveyors and the visit lasted for five days.

There was a manual published by JCI for the hospitals looking for an accreditation. More than 300 standards and 1,000 measurement elements for accreditation were listed in the manual. Interpretation of these standards was sometimes difficult. Hospitals sent staff to attend workshops to learn the details of JCI requirement and organized mock surveys to prepare for the site visit.

In 2006, Wan Fang was accredited by JCI. A smaller regional hospital in Taiwan was accredited one week before Wan Fang. Wan Fang was the first medical centre in Taiwan to be accredited.

By taking part in the JCI survey, staff at Wan Fang understood how to improve hospital quality to an international standard. This knowledge could hardly be learned in such detail from other methods.

Being a superintendent in a medical centre was not an easy job. Equivalent to the joint position of both chief executive officer and chief medical officer in an American hospital, the superintendent was in charge of everything. He had to be responsible for the finances, patient care, teaching, research, public relations, purchasing, logistics, personnel and legal issues; he reported regularly to the board and president of the university and to the city government. There were endless meetings to chair or to attend. Except in emergency, I did not ask my staff to work overtime, but I stayed in the hospital until very late.

Top priority on my agenda was quality improvement. Soon after I took office, Wan Fang started to prepare for JCI reaccreditation, which was conducted every three years.

Patient safety was the item most emphasized during the survey. The requirements were simple but no deviation was allowed. Specific areas included identification of patients correctly, washing hands to prevent infection, repeating the verbal instructions and writing them down to avoid misinterpreted orders, making sure to operate on the right body site of a patient, storing high risk medications carefully, and reducing the harm from falling down of patients.

It was estimated that more than 20% of patients admitted to a hospital suffered from adverse effects caused by their medical treatment. A quarter of a million Americans died of iatrogenic, or medicine-induced causes, every year. Many of them were avoidable. This was why the JCI was so concerned with patient safety.

A tracer method was widely used by the JCI during the on-site survey. The experience of a few selected patients in the hospital was traced to assess the hospital's compliance with JCI standards. This method also evaluated the hospital systems in providing care and service. By doing so, the survey process became more patient-centered. It was the view from the perspective of patients, rather than the department-oriented or function-specific approach, that the JCI would address in the survey.

There were hundreds of documents to be prepared; many of them had to be translated into English. They all had to be accurate, updated and implemented. JCI accreditation was designed to demonstrate a continuous improvement of performance; a hospital was required to present process improvement programs for quality and safety. A superintendent like me who took part in a JCI accreditation was aware of all the key issues in improving his hospital.

Many hospitals in China were trying to improve their quality. They sent their staff to Wan Fang to see how to do it. I had many opportunities to receive these guests and ask my colleagues to transfer our knowledge to them as much as possible. Some of them, such as the Second Affiliated

Hospital of Zhejiang University School of Medicine in Hangzhou, successfully passed JCI accreditation after frequent exchanges with us. For them, a Taiwanese hospital was a much easier source for collecting information, because Taiwanese and Chinese spoke the same language and shared much common culture.

Shuang-Ho Hospital was opened at the time I was appointed superintendent of Wan Fang. It was the third teaching hospital of Taipei Medical University. The government provided land to the university in the southern suburb of Taipei. The university was responsible for the building and operation of the hospital. Fifty years later, the building and all equipment would be transferred to the government. The successful story of Taipei Medical University's management of Wan Fang Hospital was the main reason behind the university's successful bid for this project from the government.

Chiu was the inaugural superintendent of the Shuang-Ho Hospital, which was mainly designed by him. I was asked by the board of the university to mobilize resources in Wan Fang to support the operation of Shuang-Ho. Senior doctors, residents, nurses, technicians and administrative staff were rotated to this sister hospital. Newly hired staff there learned the standard operating procedures from Wan Fang for preparing hospital accreditation in Taiwan and JCI from abroad. Everything was smoothly completed. I managed to maintain a healthy growth without financial setback in Wan Fang, even though many resources were drained towards Shuang-Ho. For a novice hospital superintendent, that was not a bad performance.

CHAPTER 27

Law and Ethics.
Financial Numbers and Human Resources.

became a better medical doctor after being a superintendent of a hospital. That could be ironic, but it was definitely true. The main reason I say so was that I learned to see the doctor-patient relationship not only from the doctor's side but also from the patient's.

The medical education I received emphasized the technical aspects of medicine. We were taught that if we could diagnose and treat patients well, patients would appreciate and follow our instructions. In other words, if we provided a good service, patients would buy it. In a market where demand exceeded supply, the buyer did not have much to choose. The patients had few options but to obey the doctors.

The world had been changed radically. In a modern age of information, a layman has relatively easy access to medical knowledge. It was the explosion of information that confused the patients, not the lack of it. Very few of them would be satisfied with a straightforward order from the doctor; they wanted to know the rationale behind the decision of their doctor. Even if they silently received a prescription, they would leave with many questions in their mind. Trust in a doctor was no more a patient's reflex; it had to be earned by the doctor. Distrust in a doctor, however, could be easily inflamed by those surrounding the patient.

Among my duties as a superintendent in the hospital, one of the most serious was handling malpractice accusations against hospital staff. Every month, I had a meeting with senior medical doctors, legal advisors, social workers, the personnel officer and the public relationship manager to review every serious complaint by patients or their families. Most cases could be solved before going to the court, but we did have several litigations that were time-consuming and morally depressing.

We had a very good lawyer to give us advice. He was fair and always told us honestly if we had done something inappropriate. In such cases, we should admit our mistakes and give compensation to the injured.

In many cases, the reason a patient was so unsatisfied that he filed a complaint asking for compensation was not a technical one, but a communication one. The patient had misunderstood the doctor, who did not communicate well with the patient. The patient thought that the doctor did not fulfil the promise either given or hinted by the doctor to the patient during their interaction. A signed written consent did not waive the doctor from responsibilities; a patient could easily dispute many issues that were only vaguely defined on the paper.

Attitude was another reason for resentment. Patients or their family members could be so angry that they threatened to disclose to the public how they were poorly treated in the hospital. A minor dissatisfaction could be developed into a serious confrontation. Almost in every case, they were unhappy not solely because of the incident, but because of the attitude of the hospital staff in handling the incident.

Patients might express their complaints by telephone, letter or e-mail to the hospital. I had an assistant to read all these complaints and prepare to answer them. Individual staff who were complained about would receive a copy and were asked to give an explanation. Department heads of staff would also be notified of the complaint. I periodically reviewed these cases. I heard the voice of the patients, but not all of them. For every patient who filed a complaint, there were many others who did not express their dissatisfaction but shared the same feelings.

On rare occasions, some patients or their families tried to take advantage of the hospital. When I had just taken office, an elderly lady with multiple diseases died in the intensive care unit. Her family refused to take her body back from the hospital and claimed that our doctors did not treat their patient well. They asked for a certain amount of cash as compensation. I called a meeting and found nothing wrong with our management in this case. The hospital refused the request of the family.

Soon I received a telephone call threatening to harm me physically if I did not pay a ransom. The caller did not mention that he had anything to

Law and Ethics. Financial Numbers and Human Resources.

159

do with that case; he only said that he was a man wanted by police and short of money. That was a typical practice of the Taiwanese Mafia; I knew their trick well. My father was threatened several times when he was a medical practitioner. Medical doctors in small clinics were easy targets for these rogues; big hospitals could also be blackmailed.

We notified the police; several local politicians who were well connected told them that the whole drama was played out by the local Mafia who liked to test whether I, the new superintendent, was weak and naive. We also let the family know if they had any questions regarding the cause of death, we would ask for an autopsy. They soon moved the body out of the hospital and buried her. In Taiwan, no children could accept an autopsy on their parents unless the elderly expressed their will to do so when they were still alive.

The elder generation of Taiwanese doctors was taught to save every life, regardless of the will of the patients, or that of their legal representatives if they were unable to express their will. It was common to see a fleet of life-sustaining machines including respirators, infusion pumps, monitors, wires and tubes applied to a terminally ill patient who had little chance of recovery.

Only in recent years, did hospices start to be accepted by patients and their families in Taiwan. The government officially encouraged patients to sign a Do Not Resuscitate document whilst they still could express their wills. This legal form ordered the medical staff to withhold resuscitation in case the heart stopped beating. Dying in dignity was a vital part of patient care. A terminal patient dying lonely in an isolated room in the intensive care unit surrounded by machines instead of family and friends was miserable.

'Respect the choice of a patient' is now the most important principle of medical ethics. That was never taught to medical students of my generation. When I was studying at medical school, medical ethics were given to us by clergymen who volunteered to teach in the class. Students were expected to behave like saints, which was difficult to follow.

Every month, I organized a seminar on legal and ethical issues in medical practice for students and young doctors. They would present cases with legal or ethical dilemmas and discuss with me in a group. I guided them in the principles and logics of a sound doctor-patient relationship. What they learned most from me was to see each case from the patient's perspective.

Humanistic education was essential during a medical doctor's development. Most medical students came from middle-class families, well protected by parents, attended good schools and shared a common lifestyle with their peers. They knew little about the world outside their daily routines. If they did not have the life experience of patients who came from every corner of the society, how could they communicate well with these patients, understand them and have empathy with them?

Humanism could only be developed through an education in humanities. History, literature and philosophy broaden the mind and scope of young medical students. Once they realized the importance of humanities in medicine, they would continue to pursue them during their life, think independently and intellectually in their careers, and not practise only their technical skills like craftsmen.

Acting as the vice-president of Taipei Medical University, I organized a course on Literature in Medicine for pre-med students. In the classroom, we read masterpieces written by Chinese and foreign authors and discussed the medical issues mentioned in these works. Students were asked to write a paper at the end of the semester. I was moved by some students who spent a great deal of effort in preparing their assignment; I chose to read many books which they recommended to me.

I was happy to know that several senior faculties, both at the Taipei Medical University and other medical schools in Taiwan, stood up to promote medical humanism. Mainstream medical education had shifted from an authoritative model to a patient-centered one.

After serving as an executive in various positions, I realized that lawyers and accountants were extremely helpful in management. The most important lesson I learned from the lawyers was to check the documents: words talked. From the accountants, I learned to read the numbers: numbers counted.

I insisted on seeing the written documents, rather than listen to the interpretation of my staff when an argument was raised. Very often, a decision could be easily made when the source documents were read.

Few medical doctors knew accountancy. I developed an interest in it after reading some business books at Boston. With a computer, I learned to prepare income statements, balance sheets, cashflow, and analyze their inter-relationship. No matter where I was serving, at Genelabs, Sinogen, Taipei Medical University or Wan Fang, I enjoyed discussions with accountants who provided me with inside information based on numbers they prepared. It was true that financial numbers were subject to interpretation; however, they were essential tools; without them a decision could hardly be made comfortably.

Ann, my elder daughter, became a lawyer while Wan the younger became an accountant. I did not push them towards a medical career.

The job of a superintendent was done through his staff, not by the man himself. It was people that made a difference. According to *Winning*, a book written by Jack Welch the former CEO of General Electric, human resources was the most important department in a company. It should recruit, train and retain the best staff. *Winning* gave me invaluable inspiration during my tenure as a superintendent. It was the number one *Wall Street Journal* bestseller and considered as the ultimate business how-to book.

The most sought-after character of a member of staff was innovation. Described in his book *Re-imagine*, Tom Peters called for an exploration of radical ways to overcome outdated business models and embrace aggressive strategies to empower talents. Peter wrote *In Search of Excellence* in the 1980s, one of the biggest-selling business books ever. *Re-imagine*, published in 2003, was a passionate call to wake up not only the business world, but education and society as well. I would recommend it strongly to anyone who likes to know how the future should be managed.

I appointed new heads in more than half the divisions and departments at Wan Fang Hospital. Some of them were promoted, while others were replaced by more energetic and enthusiastic young staff. A simple criterion to judge whether a clinical department was running well was to see if the patients were normally distributed among doctors in the department. If the majority of patients were treated by the chief while his colleagues had few patients, he was most likely a poor leader who took little care of his department. In departments that showed such an ominous sign, only the chief enjoyed an enviable financial reward while his colleagues were poorly paid. All these departments were losing money in their operations. The same applied to politics; if the wealth of a nation was owned by the highest-ranking officer of the government, this nation was in trouble.

I only served a three-year-term as superintendent. Aged more than 60, I was physically and mentally unfit to continue such a heavy responsibility. Fei-Peng Lee, professor of otolaryngology, succeeded the position I left.

Wen-Ta Chiu left Taipei Medical University to become the Minister of

Health in the government. Yun Yen was appointed by the board as the new president of the university. Yen was an oncologist. After completing his medical degree at Taipei Medical College, he went to the United States to obtain a PhD and receive clinical training. He spent most of his career at the City of Hope Cancer Centre in Los Angeles, California. When he was a medical student, he was editor-in-chief of the student journal; I did the same job several years before him.

Many new leaders at Taipei Medical University were younger than me. They were capable, decent and hard-working. I was very glad that the university had so many talents that I only needed to fulfil my function as a doctor and a teacher. After all, to be a good doctor and teacher are my core values. Management is interesting, but only a sidetrack for me.

CHAPTER 28

Health and Disease.
The Doctor as a Patient.

With little gray hair, I looked young for my age; not many knew that I took a lot of medicine to keep healthy. I was taking all kinds of drugs on which I did research when I was young. Several times I told a patient who did not take medication regularly that I took more pills than him. I learned to be a good doctor partly by being a patient.

Other than a runny nose, cough, toothache and indigestion, I had suffered from no less than 15 diseases, most of them were acute, some of them chronic.

When I was studying at elementary school, I was hospitalized after I was hit by a car.

As a second-year medical student, I was infected with acute hepatitis after coming back from camping on a beach.

In London, I got facial palsy and herpes zoster; both were considered as a reactivation of the herpes virus in my body.

Working as an attending physician at Taipei Veterans General Hospital, I experienced a sudden hearing loss that left me with a permanent hearing impairment in my left ear.

In Shenzhen, China, I experienced my first attack of severe lower back pain. After it, I had several further attacks.

As vice-president of Taipei Medical University, I was sent to the emergency department for treatment of renal colic.

I was admitted for herpangina with tens of ulcers in my throat. It was so painful that I could not swallow my own saliva. Morphine was given to relieve pain and intravenous fluid supplied my water and nutrients. My first swallow of an iced drink after several days' order of 'nil by mouth' was the most delicious taste I can remember.

In winter days, I suffered from a frozen shoulder. Movement of my left arm was limited by pain. My symptoms were completely relieved after Ming-Shium Hsieh, professor of orthopedics and director of the medical school, gave me a local injection of steroids. Hsieh shared many experiences with me. He was my classmate at medical school. His father, like mine, was a medical doctor. We both lost our fathers soon after we graduated from medical school. He and I were the only two among 125 classmates who had been educated in Europe; he studied for several years in Germany. We were also the only two in the class that returned to our alma mater and became full professors. He was a very busy academic surgeon; we worked closely to reform the curriculum for medical students.

During a routine physical checkup, I was found to have silent gallstones and hyperlipidemia. I took statins to lower my cholesterol level, as did many of my patients.

My blood pressure became elevated two years after I served as the superintendent at Wan Fang Hospital. I regularly took drugs to control it. It was well documented that some anti-hypertensive drugs had a protective effect on the kidneys of diabetic patients.

I visited Wan, my younger daughter, during the Christmas vacation at Cambridge, where she was studying. I walked along the Cam River; it was freezing and snowing. Returning to Taipei, I had bad flu, which developed into pneumonia. This infection was resolved only after I took antibiotics continuously for a week.

The most serious disease I had was diabetes. My parents were not diabetic. My maternal grandmother had mild diabetes and one of her sons died of diabetic complications during middle age.

As a staff member at Taipei Veterans General Hospital, every year I received a physical checkup at the hospital. Aged 45 I was told for the first time that my blood sugar was borderline high. I asked the opinion from Shih-Tzer Tsai, my classmate at medical school and one of the top diabetologists in Taiwan. He suggested that I have a glucose tolerance test, in which glucose in my blood was measured repeatedly after I drank several glasses of sugar water. He concluded that I had diabetes and advised me to start dietary therapy.

Health and Disease. The Doctor as a Patient.

165

I gained 10kg after returning from London to Taipei, I added a further 5kg when I returned from Boston. Being overweight was strongly associated with diabetes.

Two years later, Tsai suggested I take oral drugs to control my blood sugar. The drug dose was increased year by year. By the time I started my job as a superintendent at the Wan Fang Hospital, I began to inject insulin into my abdominal skin every day. It was 14 years after I was first told I had diabetes. The insulin I used was recombinant, not insulin extracted from animals. The design of the syringe and needle was convenient to use and almost painless to inject.

Before I started insulin treatment, I was given a newly marketed oral hypoglycemic drug called pioglitazone. A few months later, I noticed edema in my ankles, then I was awakened at night because of sudden shortness of breath. I had to sit up to relieve my difficult breathing. As a cardiologist, I diagnosed myself to have early heart failure with water retention in my body. Diabetic experts at Wan Fang Hospital immediately stopped my pioglitazone. All my symptoms subsided. Pioglitazone was a drug of the new class glitazone. Rosiglitazone, a drug of the same class, was withdrawn in most countries in the world. The drug company that marketed rosiglitazone paid a US$3bn fine in the USA for unlawful activities, including withholding data on adverse drug effects during clinical trials of rosiglitazone. In the USA and the UK, pioglitazone was only allowed to be sold with a warning on the packet.

Heart disease was one of the worst complications for diabetic patients; it could be life-threatening. I would never take glitazone again or give it to my patients. There were many better options for the treatment of diabetes.

Some doctors suggested patients check blood sugar at home in order to adjust the drug dose. This was only indicated to some patients, whose diabetes was poorly controlled.

In Chinese, diabetes mellitus was called a disease of sugar in urine. In most patients who had normal kidneys to excrete sugar in the urine, urine sugar was a good indicator of blood sugar. A daily check of urine sugar was an alternative to daily blood sugar measurement. I checked my urine sugar every morning for more than a decade.

When my urine sugar was abnormally high, most likely I had consumed some food rich in sugar. I could adjust my drug dose accordingly and avoid taking the specific food with high sugar content in the future.

Sugar is the number one enemy to public health in modern society. Sugar-containing drinks, pastries and cookies are temptations to children and adults alike. Being overweight is endemic in developed as well as developing countries; sugar plays the most important role in becoming overweight. The medical costs of dealing with being overweight and its complications are soaring around the world. I regret that I did not know how bad sugar was for my health when I was young. To every patient of mine I advise them to avoid sweet food and drink.

As a patient, I learned the uncertainty of medicine. A good example was my experience of facial palsy.

At Blackwells Bookshop on Broad Street in Oxford, I first found that I could not read clearly and close my eyelids as I had intended. I also noticed that one side of my cheek was paralyzed. I diagnosed facial palsy for myself and immediately went to seek assistance.

The 50th anniversary of the British Pharmacological Society was held in Oxford. Many experts in drug treatment had gathered there. I met a professor of statistics whom I had known previously. He advised me to take steroids because a clinical trial showed that patients treated with steroids recovered better than those without and the difference was statistically significant. Then I met Mark Chaput de Saintonge, a consultant at St. Bartholomew's Hospital who co-authored my first paper. He advised me not to take the drug, because most patients would recover uneventfully. He said that steroids were beneficial only to a small number of patients; there was no need to risk the side effects of steroid treatment. The difference between those with and without steroid treatment was statistically significant but not clinically significant, he commented critically.

In the evening, I met Professor Turner and asked him what I should do. He smiled to me and said, why not take a half dose? He wrote a prescription for me to buy steroid tablets at the pharmacy. I only took a few of them to relieve my anxiety.

There are always pros and cons to medical decisions. Sometimes, benefits clearly outweigh any harm done, but this is not always the case. Guidelines prepared by experts are widely used for medical doctors in the management of patients, but there are still many grey areas. Nowadays, doctors are advised to tell patients the benefits and side effects of all treatment options and let patients take part in making a decision. Informed consent, or informed choice, becomes a standard medical practice of the modern age.

Health and Disease. The Doctor as a Patient.

167

Complementary and alternative medicine or CAM in short, is becoming more and more popular all over the world. Homeopathy, yoga, aromatherapy, and magnetic healing are examples of CAM. Traditional Chinese medicine including acupuncture and herbal drugs is considered as a branch of CAM in America and Europe. Nowadays, many mainstream medical schools teach CAM to their students; and a large number of hospitals provide various types of CAM therapy to their patients.

Even though I was once a director of an institute of traditional medicine and published several research papers on Chinese herbal drugs, I never gave CAM therapy to my patients. I myself had likewise never been treated with CAM until I had several episodes of severe lower back pain.

In most cases, lower back pain without anatomical lesions is caused by muscle strain. Poor posture is an important precipitating factor. In the first few days of an attack, even a small movement of the legs is unbearable. Drugs and rehabilitation give only partial relief. It takes several days before symptoms are alleviated.

One morning, I was at work in the office of the vice-president at Taipei Medical University. All of a sudden I suffered from an acute attack of lower back pain. From my experience of previous attacks, I knew I had to cancel my activities, take analgesics, rest on the bed and wear a waist support. Nothing was more effective than waiting for a few days to achieve recovery.

A colleague suggested I visit the department of traditional Chinese medicine at the university hospital on campus. He told me that acupuncture was quite effective to relieve lower back pain. He had personal experience and strongly recommended his doctor of Chinese medicine to me. Taipei Medical University did not provide undergraduate degrees in traditional Chinese medicine, but we had a department of Chinese medicine in all our teaching hospitals where qualified doctors of Chinese medicine treated patients with acupuncture and herbal drugs.

I followed the colleague to the clinic where two acupuncture needles were inserted into my body, one in my loin, the other in the back of my hand. A weak electric current was applied to the needles. A few minutes later, I felt my back relax. To my great surprise, I was able to stand up from the bed smoothly soon after completing a treatment course of around 20 minutes. I could walk and I attended a dinner party that evening.

There were several well-designed clinical trials showing the beneficial effect of acupuncture on lower back pain. Many of them were undertaken in Germany where acupuncture was widely practiced. Claude Wit, a female professor at Berlin University, was instrumental in promoting scientific research on acupuncture. I invited her to visit Taiwan to share with us her experience in acupuncture research.

My first treatment with acupuncture was amazing. But the effect of acupuncture was less prominent during my subsequent attacks of lower back pain, particularly when the pain was associated with flu.

In the last year of my service as a superintendent, I began to suffer from irregular heartbeats, commonly known as arrhythmia. During the worst episodes, one in every five beats was ectopic. Fortunately a thorough examination of my heart found no other abnormalities. In many patients, irregular heart rhythm was a manifestation of their underlying heart disease, such as coronary atherosclerosis or myocardial ischemia. I had to be very cautious because I had several risk factors for heart disease such as old age, diabetes, hypertension and hypercholesterolemia.

Another risk factor for me was that I had smoked in the past. I learned to smoke a pipe in London, later shifting to cigars when I found it too warm to hold a pipe in Taiwan. I quit smoking several years ago. Before that I only smoked once or twice a month; I was never a heavy smoker. Smoking is definitely detrimental to health in those who smoke; it is also harmful to those who involuntarily become passive smokers.

The symptoms of arrhythmia annoyed me so I took cardiac drugs to suppress them. Sometimes a sedative drug also relieved palpitation; this indicated my arrhythmia was related to mental stress.

I had constantly faced stressful conditions in my life, as many readers of this book can understand.

For years, I suffered from irritable bowel syndrome with intermittent abdominal pain and alternating diarrhea and constipation. This disorder is known to be associated with stress.

Exhausted by stressful work, I felt blue from time to time. Fumi noticed that my emotions were cyclic and reached their worst at the end of each month. Since then, I paid special attention to cheering myself up to prevent this periodic fall in mood.

When I was young, I had frequent attacks of aphthous ulcers. This was a painful ulcer in the mouth, lasting for around two weeks. It recurred again and again, worse if I was under stress or lacking sleep. Steroid ointment, a standard therapy recommended by many doctors, only partially relieved the symptoms. It was interesting that I had few attacks in England, where I learned to eat yogurt. Even if it recurred after I returned to Taiwan, it was milder in severity and the clinical course shortened if I took lactobacilli at the start of symptom. Yogurt was rich in lactobacilli.

Recently, a new theory claimed that abnormal growth of intestinal bacteria could be responsible for some types of chronic disease such as diabetes, atherosclerosis and immunological disorders. Lactobacillus, which had previously been given to patients with indigestion, was promoted recently as a food supplement to keep people healthy. Lactobacillus was supposed to modify the growth of intestinal bacteria. Many papers containing innovative research on this subject were published in top-tier scientific journals. If this theory was proved true, medicine would be revolutionized. In the last century, bacteria outside the body were considered the main causes of diseases; in the next century, those inside the body could be far more important. I like to keep an eye on the future development of this interesting subject.

It is true that we should not stick to a dogma. What we once believed as true could only be an illusion. The history of science and medicine has repeatedly taught us this lesson. Elevated sugar in blood might only be a part of the disease called diabetes. We measured blood sugar to diagnose diabetes, simply because sugar was easy to test. Blood sugar, like blood pressure or blood cholesterol, was only a surrogate marker of a chronic disease. There could be other body changes more fundamental to these diseases.

The last PhD student I supervised was Chun-Feng Huang; a young doctor specializing in family medicine. Using a metabolomics approach, he found that urine nicotinuric acid was elevated in his patients with diabetes and metabolic syndrome which included being overweight, hypertension and hyperlipidemia. Nicotinuric acid was the major metabolic product of nicotinic acid, involved in lipid metabolism and insulin resistance. He proposed that nicotinuric acid represented an important pathogenic mechanism in the process from metabolic syndrome to diabetes and atherosclerosis. We published this research in 2013 in *Diabetes Care*. Someday, a doctor might order a urine nicotinuric acid test to see if your diabetes and atherosclerosis are improving. Who knows?

As a patient and a doctor, I learned to live with chronic diseases; I taught patients to live with them. Until medical scientists made a new breakthrough, these chronic diseases would continue to spread among us; they could only be partially controlled but not totally eradicated.

In my heart as a curious scientist, I expect someday a great medical discovery will radically change the way we understand, diagnose and treat common but potentially serious chronic diseases. Breakthroughs in medicine will occur following innovative and curiosity-driven research. Research is the cornerstone of medical progress. Every generation should support medical research for the benefits of themselves and for those coming in the future.

CHAPTER 29

National Health Insurance in Taiwan. Treat a Patient, Not Just a Disease.

Taiwan started a national health insurance scheme in 1994. Every legal resident, including foreigners working here, was covered. For most citizens, the employer paid 60% of the premium, the employee 30% and the government 10%. Co-payment for an outpatient visit to a local clinic was around US$3-5; for a visit to a large hospital, it ranged between US$10-20, including drugs and laboratory tests. The ceiling for a co-payment in one hospitalization was around US$1,000, no matter how complicated the disease was. Those suffering financial hardship could apply to waive the premium and the co-payment. Co-payment for certain severe diseases such as cancer could also be waived.

Before the implementation of national health insurance, only 60% of the population was covered by various types of insurances which were provided to employed workers, farmers, veterans, soldiers, teachers, and those serving in government.

The population in Taiwan was 23 million; annual income was US$21,000 per person. Taiwan spent around seven percent of its gross domestic product on healthcare. This number was relatively low as compared with 15% in USA or 10% in most European countries.

There were 400 hospitals with a total bed capacity of 160,000. Besides, there were 11,000 medical clinics all over the island. The ratio of doctor to population was 1:400. Thirteen medical colleges produce 1,500 medical doctors a year. There were some young Taiwanese who studied at medical schools abroad, mostly in southeast Asia, Eastern Europe or South America.

Returning to Taiwan, they were allowed to practice medicine if they could pass a series of examinations. However, those who studied at medical schools in China were not allowed to do so because their diploma from Chinese schools was not recognized by Taiwanese government as being equivalent to a diploma from Taiwanese medical schools.

Medical service in Taiwan was highly esteemed internationally. It was not only efficient and convenient but also cheap for the quality provided. It has repeatedly been ranked among the best healthcare systems in the world by organizations such as the Economist Intelligent Unit. An important factor that contributed to low medical costs in Taiwan was the relatively low salary paid to medical professionals including doctors, nurses and other technical staff. Economic policy in Taiwan was typically capitalistic, while medical service in Taiwan was extremely socialist. The government controlled every aspect of medical practice, service charges in particular, through the national health insurance reimbursement scheme. Since private medical insurance was not popular, National Health Insurance Administration in the government was practically the only payer in healthcare.

Patients could change easily their doctor and hospital if they were not satisfied with the original ones. Access to medical care was very convenient except in mountain areas and isolated islands.

A side-effect of such a system was a tendency to 'hospital shop' among patients. They received repeat examinations and duplicate drugs from various doctors at different hospitals. Application of information technology to prevent such a waste had just started.

Fees for service, rather than fees for quality, were the basic principle in reimbursing the hospitals and medical doctors. Since service providers were encouraged to do more under such a system, abuse and waste were inevitable.

Another problem was over-specialization. More than 70% of medical doctors were specialists. Most patients sought specialists to treat their aliments without referral. The function of primary care doctors as gate keepers did not exist, even though in theory it was encouraged. Many patients with multiple diseases visited several specialists at the same time; each specialist managed a specific disease. Medical centres were packed with patients; specialists could only give a few minutes to each patient in their clinics. Medical doctors were overworked while patients often got only fragmented care.

A referral system might be difficult to implement in Taiwan, because the general public are used to easy access to specialists in hospitals. The only force that could change the practice of medicine in Taiwan would be a demand for quality. Future patients would not tolerate long waiting times followed by a brisk interaction with their doctors. They would ask for comprehensive medical care, similar to that given by doctors in developed countries, rather than a refill of a prescription from the doctor soon after seeing them.

Future generations of medical doctors would also demand better quality in their practice; they could not be pushed any more to see a large number of patients, resulting in superficial doctor-patient relationships making medical careers seem unattractive.

There was a call to emphasize holistic care in medicine. During periodic inspection of medical schools by the Ministry of Education in Taiwan, the way students were taught to take care of a patient as a whole was critically evaluated. Medical curriculums were reformed to reduce the time spent in teaching technical details for rare diseases; more resources were allocated to the teaching of general medicine, which was essential for all medical doctors taking care of patients. Rare diseases were learned during specialist training after medical school.

A teaching clinic was designed at Wan Fang Hospital to provide general medical education in an ambulatory setting for medical students and junior medical doctors. Every week, I spent half a day in this clinic teaching a small group of students how to take detailed medical history, perform complete physical examinations, arrange various laboratory tests, make a tentative diagnosis and give treatments accordingly. Less than six patients were seen in each session. We would spend a minimum of 45 minutes on a new patient and 15 minutes on a follow-up meeting; much longer than the time spent on patients by average Taiwanese doctors, including me in my regular clinic. Such a teaching clinic had been set up in several medical centres in Taiwan, as requested by the hospital accreditation committee. I strongly supported this type of education and actively took part in it.

The American College of Physicians endowed me a fellowship in 2007. I attended the annual meeting of the college in Washington DC to receive this honor. From then on, I could proudly put the title FACP after my name. It was equivalent to a FRCP, Fellow of the Royal College of Physicians in the UK. For a physician outside the United States who did not receive clinical training in an American hospital, this was an unusual recognition of his contribution to internal medicine. I fully endorsed the mission statements of the college and regularly updated my knowledge in every aspect of internal medicine through the continuous medical education programs provided by the college. It was the best medical professional organization I had ever known.

When I was a medical student, I saw many patients who declined treatment for financial reasons. They had neither a job nor insurance. Since the start of the national health insurance scheme, there were no such miseries in Taiwan. I recently heard stories about American families broken by unbearable medical expenses. To me it was unacceptable that a country as rich as America had such a healthcare system, ignoring the needs of the less privileged.

Year on year, I became more and more religious. I did not join any religious organization and rarely attended religious activities, but I was awed by the supernatural and felt humble in front of the almighty.

The traditional Chinese religion was a mixture of Buddhism, Taoism and Confucianism. Buddhism is a philosophy of life and death originating in India. Taoism the worship of nature and spirits; it has been practised in China for thousands of years. Confucianism is a discipline for daily life that follows the sayings of Confucius.

I had been exposed to the teachings of several religions. When I first listened to Bach's St. Matthew Passion in London, I was very much moved, even though I was not a Christian. Many times, including the day my father passed away, my sorrow could only be partially relieved by listening to the sutra sung by nuns. I prayed for forgiveness when I was touched by the simple but thoughtful sayings of religious sages.

I respected those who had their own religion, and never tried to persuade others to follow mine. Religion is very personal. Certain unexpected but significant incidents at critical moments of life strengthened one's faith to religion. Respecting such untold but sacred memories of others should be the basis for religious tolerance.

Mercy is the highest virtue of all religions. Without the mercy of the almighty and that of many others, we would suffer more in our destinies. Medicine without mercy is unsustainable. There are occasions in a medical career when only mercy can keep a doctor away from indifference.

I remember clearly Christmas in London, 1981. Fumi returned to

Taipei; I rented a room in the Nuffield College of the Royal College of Surgeons at Lincoln's Inn Fields, London to write my PhD thesis. Breakfast and dinner were provided at this accommodation. However, the catering service was suspended during Christmas. Knowing that I was alone, Turner advised me to have lunch with on-duty staff at the medical ward of which he was in charge.

It was snowing heavily; all transport including the Tube and buses were suspended. I walked to the hospital; fortunately it was not far away.

When I entered the ward, I was surprised to see Turner, with his wife and daughter, in a chef's white hat and gown serving lunch to patients who were unable to return home for Christmas. He must have driven a long way in that terrible weather from his house in Ascot. On working days, he usually took the train to the hospital.

I was not sure if what Turner did for his patients was common among British doctors. It was my understanding that there was no need for him to flatter his patients, ordinary people in a National Health Service hospital. He must have done it for years but few in the department knew. Long after I had passed through many stages of my medical career, I still remembered that day Turner taught me the most important lesson in medicine. From Turner, I learned not only his research, which was eventually over; I was also privileged to learn his compassion, which was ever-lasting.

CHAPTER 30

Learning from the Young.
Interest in Medical History.

T here was a Taiwanese named Kai-Shek Hsieh. He was born in 1878 when Taiwan was ruled by the empire of Qing Dynasty in China. He became a Japanese subject when Taiwan was ceded to Japan. After studying law in Japan, he served as the Minister of Foreign Affairs for the Manchuria State. He was sent to prison by the government of the Republic of China after Japanese surrender. Communists released him when the People's Republic of China was established. He died in 1954 in Beijing.

During his life, he had five nationalities: Qing, Japan, Manchuria, Republic of China and People's Republic of China. Many of them were not his choice. Albeit an extreme example, his experience of an identification crisis was nevertheless shared by many Taiwanese. They had difficulty knowing which country they belonged to. Flags to which they pledged allegiance were put into the trash of history. They learned to be skeptical about the rhetoric of patriotism, which was mostly enforced rather than drawn from their instinct. They, however, were proud to be Taiwanese, since they had collectively overcome the misfortune and injustice imposed upon them.

Taiwanese were not heroic or fearless; on the other hand, they tried to avoid direct confrontation as much as possible. Except for those who were less educated, few Taiwanese were stubborn. Most of the time, they were flexible and willing to negotiate. These characteristics were essential for them to survive in difficulties, particularly in a territory where they had just landed.

Taiwanese carried the gene of unrest from their ancestors; they had an inherited trait of migration. Taiwanese were the most mobile among the

Chinese. Chinese history started along the banks of Yellow River in northern China. Most Chinese stayed in their hometowns; only a few moved southwards. Among those who crossed the Yangtze River and settled down in the fertile farmland, a small group left and moved further to the hilly Fukien Province. Some in Fukien migrated to Quanzhou on the coast. From there, the adventurous ones crossed the strait and immigrated to Taiwan. It could be concluded that it was the most outward-looking Chinese that came to Taiwan. There were many reasons for them to move; seeking a better place to live and to raise their children was certainly one of them, but I guessed that intolerance to the commonplace could also have been a strong motivation.

Taiwanese businessmen carried suitcases packed with samples, travelling alone to remote corners of the globe to sell their products made at home. A tiny island with no natural resources, Taiwan rose to become the 19th biggest economic power in the world. People of my generation contributed to the tremendous progress of Taiwan from post-war poverty into a prosperous country. I myself was able to enjoy the sweet fruit of success after a life of hard work. Everything surrounding me was moving in a positive direction.

As a professional, I developed my career from a bumpy start to a smooth course. Throughout my career, I retained my core values: to be a good doctor and teacher, never betraying the Oath of Hippocrates.

I love my family. I could not have a better life were I not married to Fumi. I regretted that I did not give her as much as I should have. Our daughters are lovely and charming; Ann is always calm and brave, Wan clever and sweet.

My alma mater medical school had grown from a local college to an internationally renowned university. QS World University Ranking, based in London put it among the 100 best universities in the world to study medicine. Only seven universities in UK, six in Asia and 20 in the USA were ranked better than Taipei Medical University in 2014. The total number of medical schools in the world was around 2,000.

The small hospital on the campus where I served as one of its first eight residents became a centre of medical excellence. TMU Health Care System, with a total capacity of 3,000 beds, was one of the largest healthcare providers in metropolitan Taipei.

The Taiwanese enjoyed not only an impressive economic growth but also a democratic civil society.

China, the homeland of my ancestors, stood up again and showed the glory of its great culture and civilization.

The relationship between Taiwan and China was smooth and peaceful. Every week, hundreds of non-stop flights carried passengers travelling between Taiwan and major cities in China. A million Taiwanese were living and/or working in China. Tourists from China flooded Taiwan. Chinese cordially considered Taiwanese their fellow citizens; although some Taiwanese who favored independence hesitated to accept this.

Looking back, I am extremely thankful. There were many who nurtured, taught, guided, assisted, supported and loved me. Some of them had known me for years, while some had only a brief encounter with me.

In spite of my satisfaction about all the progress made over the years, I was worried about the future. This could be an exaggeration of my pessimism, but I had reasons for it.

What worried me most was pollution of the environment. Human beings were abusing the globe. There were no reasons why we should live a lifestyle that wasted the limited resources of the world and deprived coming generations of their futures. Economic growth in certain parts of the world had developed so much that waste became a necessity to sustain the greedy growth. Respect for the harmony between nature and human beings had been distorted by a constant desire to conquer the nature in the name of advancement or development.

Wide use of chemicals was an example. Many chemicals and chemical wastes were rich in hormonal activities. A study in Europe found half of the fishes in a river were hermaphroditic, which meant half male and half female in one body, because the river was polluted with chemicals. The alarming increase of several types of cancer was definitely related to the unlimited and unneeded use of chemicals in daily life.

In spite of these worries, sooner or later we, the elderly, should hand over all we had to the young. No matter how smart or hard working we were, the future would be theirs and their destiny could only be their choice. Would they be doing better than us?

'Don't worry, just let us do,' Wan reminded me.

I realized the simple fact that we should let the young do their job without our interference, mainly from the knowledge I learned from my daughters, Wan in particular.

Wan was seven years younger than her sister. She finished high school

Learning from the Young. Interest in Medical History.

179

in Taiwan, studied accounting at the University of Washington in Seattle, and then worked in financial institutions including KPMG in New York.

Partly encouraged by me, she went to Cambridge in the UK for her MBA. A student at Pembroke College, she enjoyed British life more than I had. After passing an interview which was ranked by *Forbes* magazine as the toughest one for a new job, she became a consultant at the London Office of McKinsey & Company in 2011.

I trusted that she was among the young elite so I listened to her carefully; more than most fathers to their daughters. From what she was saying and doing, I knew that the younger generation was far more capable than us. They had all the advantages the modern world could afford them. They were immersed in an age of information; the knowledge they mastered was far beyond my estimation. They were sharp in analysis and prompt in execution. Their connection was global while their touch was personal.

Their value and judgement could be different from ours, some of their style and manners difficult for us to adapt fully, but they were showing us the trends of the future. I admired them. I would let them lead the world. I should stand aside.

Keeping in mind that our generation would fade away, I started to ask if anything in the past could be worth remembering. My interest in medical history was renewed, after it had hibernated in my mind for decades.

Very soon I developed a keen interest in how Western medicine transferred to China during the 19th century. To my great surprise little literature was available to record such an important historic process.

Benjamin Hobson, a British medical missionary who came to China in 1839, published five medical books in Chinese between 1851-1858. This series of books covered chemistry, physics, anatomy, physiology, drug therapy, internal medicine, surgery, obstetrics, gynecology and pediatrics. Western medical knowledge was for the first time systematically introduced into China. In the following century, five English textbooks on internal medicine were translated into Chinese, first by British and American medical missionaries, then by ethnic Chinese medical doctors. Throughout this period, textbooks translated from English were regarded as symbols of the mainstream and authority within medical communities in China.

There was little bibliographic information on these books; early translators rarely cited the source in their translation. Fascinated by the development of modern medicine in China during an age of enormous social and political changes, I started to collect rare medical books of the late 19th and early 20th centuries in China; I also ordered photocopies of the original English textbooks that were translated. Piece by piece, I found clues to fit the jigsaw puzzle. My review paper *Chinese translation of English textbooks on internal medicine from the 1850s to 1940s* was published in the *Journal of Chinese Medical Association* in 2014.

In the process of writing this paper, I found on-line digital libraries extremely helpful. Open Library, a project associated with the non-profit Internet Archive, gave free access to millions of books. As a booklover, when I was young I used to spend my spare time in the libraries of medical schools and hospitals. In the age of the internet, everyone can read a book of his choice by pushing a computer key. The database of the Open Library was well organized; detailed information of authors' works and editions were provided. Interfaces were user-friendly while downloading simple and fast. Many distinguished universities also provide a similar service to the public, but these were smaller in scale.

I was grateful to the people and organizations who volunteered to provide 'universal access to all knowledge', a mission statement of the Internet Archive. Their contribution in protecting the most powerful human heritage, books, and in promoting the growth of intellectual activities in the world was enormous.

There was no free digital library of Chinese books. I sincerely wished that the Chinese would someday digitalize every book published during the past thousand years, not just the selected ones, and make such a library accessible to anyone who would like to read them. The great heritage of China could be better preserved and recreated in the future if such a service was available.

'Read ten thousand volumes of books and travel ten thousand miles on the road' was considered by many scholars in ancient China as the ultimate goal of life. I successfully fulfilled such a wish; it was much easier in a time of mass media and jet flight.

The gene in my body that urged me to migrate ushered me to more than 40 countries in the world, 30 states in America and 20 provinces in China; it also led me to various career stages that were challenging, stimulating and rewarding. There were many encounters during the journey; many of them have been described in this book. These encounters enriched my living and made my life memorable. I could not have planned them before they happened. Fortunately, they were mostly favorable to me.

I am grateful for all my encounters. I would like to tell you the exact title of this book in my mind, 'Serendipitous encounters of a Taiwanese medical doctor in his migration among destinations of his career'. It was too long to print on the cover so I shortened it. Hope you like it and thank you for reading it.

Map 1: Eastern part of China
(Names for provinces are underlined)

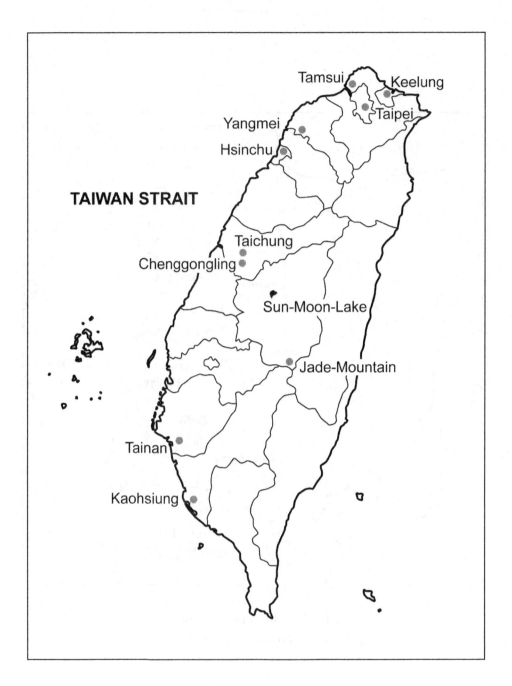

Map 2: Taiwan

CHRONOLOGY

(Corresponding chapter for each event is shown in parenthesis)

Year	Public Event	Personal Event
1624	Dutch built a fortress in Taiwan (1)	
1644	Qing Dynasty started (1)	
1661	Zeng took over Taiwan (1)	
1683	Qing emperor took over Taiwan (1)	
1839	Hobson came to China (30)	
1895	Japan took over Taiwan (1)	Grandfather visited Quanzhou (1)
1899	First medical school in Taiwan (2)	
1900	Boxer Rebellion (3)	
1904	Japan-Russia War (3)	
1912	Republic of China was founded (3)	
1931	Manchuria State was founded (3)	
1937	China-Japan War started (4)	
1939	World War II started (3)	

1945	Japan surrendered, End of World War II (2,3)	Father left Manchuria (3)
1947	228 Incident in Taiwan (4)	
1948		Parents married (4)
1949	People's Republic of China was founded (4)	Author was born (4)
1950	Korean War started (5)	
1955	Vietnam War started (6)	
1956		Father studied in USA (4)
1957		Car accident (5)
1958	Kinmen artillery battle (8)	
1960	Taipei Medical College was founded (6)	
1965	Culture Revolution in China started (6)	
1967		Freshman at Taipei Medical College (6)
1972	Nixon visited China (7)	
1974		Graduated from medical school; started military service (8)
1975	Vietnam War ended (6); President Kai-Shek Chiang died (8)	Father died (8)

1976		Married; started medical residency (9)
1977	Ze-Dong Mao died; Culture Revolution in China was over (9)	Ann was born (9)
1978	USA severed formal diplomatic tie with Taiwan (9)	
1979	Demonstration for human rights in Taiwan (10)	
1980		Started study in London (10)
1982		PhD (13); Started working at Veterans General Hospital (14)
1983		First trip to USA (14)
1984		Wan was born (14)
1986		Professor of medicine (14, 15)
1987	Taiwan lifted martial law (16)	Went to Boston (15)
1988	President Ching-Kou Chiang died (16)	Fumi founded Maxigen Enterprises (21)
1990		First visit to China (19)
1992		Director, Institute of Traditional Medicine (18); Official visit to China (19)

1994	Yang-Ming promoted to a university (20, 21); National Health Insurance started in Taiwan (29)	
1996	Taiwan Strait Crisis (20)	US patent granted (17); Sabbatical leave (20); Academic Dean (21)
1997	Hong Kong returned to China (22)	
1999	September 21 earthquake in Taiwan (22)	Started working at Genelabs (22)
2000	Sui-Pen Chen elected president (22); Taipei Medical College promoted to a university (23)	
2001	911 attacks (23)	CEO of Sinogen (23); Visited ancestors' house (24)
2003	SARS outbreak (23)	
2004		Vice President of Taipei Medical University (25)
2005		Ann got JD (21)
2007		FACP (29)
2008	In-Chow Ma elected president (22)	Ig Nobel Prize (13); Superintendent of Wan Fang Hospital (26)
2011		Wan got MBA (30)
2013		Chair Professor (18)

INDEX

Liu, Henry, 90
liver cancer, 114
liver cell culture, 114
liver cirrhosis, 42, 114
liver failure, 100
liver metabolism of drug, 73
local anesthetic effect, 69
London Hospital Medical College, 59
Longshan Temple, 5
Los Angeles, 17, 24
lupus erythematosus, 129, 130
Ma, In-Chow, 133
Macau, 30, 136
Mackay Clinic, 24
Mackay Medical College, 24, 101
Mackay Memorial Hospital, 23, 24, 101
Mackay, Captain, 24
Mackay, George, 24
Madam Chiang, Kai-Shek, 93
Madam Mau, Ze-Dong, 47
Mafia, Taiwanese, 159
Magnolia officinalis, 102
magnolol, 102
malaria, 107, 109, 125
Malaysia, 5, 30, 84
male contraceptive, 60
male infertility, 60-64, 70
malpractice, 158
Manchuria, 13, 15, 16
   State of, 15, 177
Manchuria Medical University, 15
Manchurian, 3
Mandarin Chinese, 13, 18, 20, 65, 136
Mao, Ze-Dong, 19, 36, 107, 109
   death, 47
Marco Polo, 5
marriage
   CYH and Fumi, 45
   father and mother, 18
   grandparents, 10
martial law, 20, 52, 89, 90
Massachusetts General Hospital, 81, 82,
   100

Matsu, 40
Maxigen Enterprises, Inc, 125
Mayor's Award, 24
McGill University, 42
McKinsey & Company, 180
media, 73, 79
medical curriculum, 31, 165, 174
medical ethics, 160
medical history, 180
medical license, 10
Meiji restoration, 9
membrane stabilizing activity, 69
Merck, 111
mercy, 175
metabolic syndrome, 170
metabolomics, 170
MGH, see Massachusetts General
   Hospital, 82
Michelangelo, 53, 57
microbiology, 32
micro-circulation, 95
microscope, 66
military training, 29
Ming dynasty, 3
Minister of Education, 122, 149
Minister of Finance, 78
Minister of Foreign Affairs, 53, 78, 177
Minister of Health, 162
Ministry of Education, 50, 85, 104, 147,
   148, 154, 174
Ministry of Health, 103, 125, 154
missionary, 24, 180
mitochondria, 101
molecular biology, 100
molecular cardiology, 82, 83
Moore, Joseph, 21
morphine, 164
mother, 18, 26, 32, 95, 99
Motion of the Heart and Blood, a book,
   58
murder, 90
Muslim, 72
myocardial ischemia, 62, 169

uncertainty of medicine, 167
United Nations, 47, 52
United States diplomatic relationship
    with Taiwan, 47
University College Hospital, 82
university entrance examination, 26
University of California, Berkley, 134
University of California, Davis, 114
University of California, Los Angeles,
    Centre for East-West Medicine, 115
University of California, San Diego, 78
University of Glasgow, 62, 92, 100
University of Kyoto, 11, 90
University of London, 51, 53, 58, 71
University of Michigan, 77
University of Padua, 58
University of Pennsylvania, 42
University of Texas Southwestern
    Medical Centre, 111
University of Washington, 141, 180
University Ranking, QS, 178
Upland, California, 124
urine sugar, 166
US Agency for International
    Development, 21
US Department of States, 23, 48
US Information Service, 25
vaginal absorption of drug, 73
vaginal contraceptive, 73
vaginal douche, 74
Vane, Sir John, 116
Vatican, 48, 57
venereal disease, 20, 21
Venereal Disease Control Centre, 20
ventricular premature beats, 77
venture capital, 134
vertical transmission, 114
Vesalius, Andrew, 58
VGH, see Taipei Veterans General
    Hospital, 76
vibration disease, 49
Victor Chang Cardiac Research Institute,
    84

Vietnam, 5, 94
Vietnam War, 29, 51, 107
vinegar, 137, 138
vitamin E, 102
Wallace, William, 57
Wan Fang Hospital, 146, 150, 154-157
    as superintendent in, 153, 157, 161,
    162, 164-166
    teaching clinic, 174
Wan, see Hong, Wan-Ching, 80
Wang, Fu-Mei, wife, see Fumi, 36
Wang, Nina, 127, 145
Wang, Wei-Kung, 106
Washington DC, 48, 78
Washington University, 147
Watergate scandal, 47
Webster, Grady, 114
wedding
    Ann and Henry, 124
    Charles and Diana, 70
Wei, Yau-Huei, 101
Wei-Ming Group, 135, 36, 138, 141
Welch, Jack, 162
Wellcome Research Laboratories, 63
West Lake, 108-110
White Terror, 20
White, Paul, 82
William Harvey Research Institute, 116
Winning, a book, 162
Wit, Claude, 169
World Conference of Clinical
    Pharmacology and Therapeutics, 78
World Health Organization, 20, 146
Wu, Chen-Wen, 147, 150
Wu, Chih-Hsiung, 154
Wu, Yan-Hwa, 122
Wuhan, 107
Xiamen, 5, 142
Xihu State Guesthouse, 109
Xinku, 141, 142, 144
yam, 11
Yang, Tsong-Teoh, 84
Yang-Mei, 41

CPSIA information can be obtained at www.ICGtesting.com
Printed in the USA
LVOW03s1955260315

432117LV00002B/58/P